Bet the Marking Plagued by Nits

Life coaching strategies for busy teachers

Lynette Allen

First published by

Crown House Publishing Ltd
Crown Buildings, Bancyfelin, Carmarthen, Wales, SA33 5ND, UK
www.crownhouse.co.uk

and

Crown House Publishing LLC
4 Berkeley Street, 1st Floor, Norwalk, CT 06850, USA
www.CHPUS.com

British Library Cataloguing-in-Publication Data
A catalogue entry for this book is available from the British Library.

10-digit ISBN 1845900197
13-digit ISBN 978-184590019-9

Printed and bound in the UK by
Cromwell Press, Trowbridge, Wiltshire

Contents

Personal planning action

206

A three-step strategy to make the most of precious PPA time.

About Lynette Allen

213

Plus great websites for support/resources.

Acknowledgements

Thanks to:

Caroline Lenton, Fiona Spencer Thomas, Tom Fitton and the rest of the Crown House team.

And a massive thanks to everyone who helped me with my research:

Beatrice Landucci, Tracey Allen, Annabelle Sharman, Liz Beattie, Clare Smale, Rachel Feneck, Norma Penny, Marneta Viegas, Peter Jones, Garry Burnett, Jo Somervell, Elizabeth Hughes, Kirsten Nutman, Michelle Farnworth, John Carpmael, Linda Westall, Angela Ward and Natalie Savona.

Introduction

Teaching is one of the oldest professions there is. Teachers create the foundations of society and, apart from our parents, they are our first real contact with grown-ups. Ask anyone, of any age, who their favourite teacher was, and, whatever their experience at school, you're guaranteed to hear about one very special individual who stood out above the rest. Most of us have one exceptional person we remember as trusting in our ability when everyone else thought us lazy, inarticulate or disruptive!

Etched deep in our memory, there will be one teacher we remember really connecting with, one person who helped us achieve our potential, the person who explained algebra in a language we actually understood and made chemistry seem impossibly easy. Those were the teachers who made such an impression on us that they stay with us, even in adulthood. They were the teachers we remember spending time with us, giving us extra attention when we needed it or just going that extra mile to make sure we actually 'got' whatever it was we were trying to get. Maybe school was difficult; maybe every day was a struggle; maybe you were labelled 'idle' or 'uncooperative' in the staffroom. But somehow you'd pull out all the stops to impress just that one particular teacher with whom you'd made a connection. We don't forget their advice and we don't forget the environment they worked so hard to create for us so that we could learn and develop in a safe place.

Most teachers become teachers because of their passionate desire to pass on knowledge and understanding to a brand new generation, because they love the thought of working with children and maybe even because of happy memories of their own primary school teacher.

Maybe you became a teacher because you wanted to play a vital part in the development of young minds and watch children grow into capable, self-confident teenagers and adults, making reliable decisions about their talents and future. In the twenty-first century, though, it now seems that school can be one of the toughest places to be, and carrying out all of those dreams you had before you felt the pressure of teaching gets harder and harder to do. The pressure on teachers is relentless; the demand on their time and energy is just unimaginable. Oh, if only marking and nits were the sole plague of your lives now!

We all yearn for the days when the most pressing thing on our childish mind was whether we were going to be milk monitor that day or make prefect next week! Sadly, though, there's more to deal with now than ever before, both from a teacher's point of view and from a child's perspective. There is the bullying, self-harming, eating disorders, targets, SATs – and that's just for the children! Where's the innocence gone?

If you're a teacher, you may have many of these issues to deal with at school, as well as family life, which, has its own set of complications. You may have children of your own and you'll have their education to worry about, on top of the never-ending list of chores involved in running a home. Maybe you feel as though your children aren't getting the attention from teachers you know they deserve. Yet at the same time you understand the problems completely and know that, frustratingly, you can't do a thing about it. Perhaps it's your child who's missing out on their mum because you're so busy marking and preparing lessons for other people's children.

If, by the time you're finished in the evenings and feel just about ready to spend time with them, you realise that it's bedtime and, once again, you've neglected the family mealtime, bedtime stories, bonding bathtime and, oh yes, quality time with your partner, then you'll be facing the question, 'How long can I carry on doing this?' Some of the ex-teachers I've spoken to while writing this book ended up leaving their jobs for just that reason. There are masses of inspiring, creative, passionate and wonderful teachers leaving this profession because they no longer feel able to do their job well and support a normal family life.

If that describes you and how you're feeling at the moment, and you've considered throwing in the towel despite the things you love about your job, you'll know it's time to address the real situation and deal with it head on. This is the moment to build time-saving strategies and tips into your life to make you feel more in control at home and happier and more organised at work.

I've spoken to teachers up and down the country and dug deep to expose the real goings-on in the lives of teachers, both personally and professionally, in order to create an escape valve and a handbook to help you through those difficult times.

With all the pressure of life itself, amid growing class-room numbers and demanding goals, can we really believe a classroom–life balance is attainable? The answer is yes, and the solutions are here.

This book looks at real situations with real solutions, techniques and secrets that your teaching college may have neglected to let you in on. *Behind with the Marking and Plagued by Nits* gives you easy access in short chapters to the critical information you need, when you need it. You can find the tip that relates to a particular problem or you can just close your eyes and open a page at random. You may just find the answer to a dilemma there.

If you're struggling to remember the reason you went into teaching because life's got too busy to handle, get your buzz back and trust that you teach for a reason – a very good one. Teachers don't just learn to be teachers: teaching is a way of being and, if you have that in you, you're needed in that classroom! If you're overloaded with exams, drowning under marking, feel as if you're losing yourself and there's more paper on your desk than you'll find trees in an Amazon rainforest, breathe deeply and get focused. It's time to get back to basics.

The Allen Stress Test

Before you read this book, it will be a good idea to give yourself the Allen Stress Test. It will give you a clear indication of whether you are stressed and where those particular stress spots lie in your life. You may feel as if you already know exactly what you need to do to get back on track, back to the energetic and inspiring you whom you used to see in the mirror every day. However, seeing it in black and white could just give you the push you need to address those tricky situations head on and may help you deal with things that have been wearing you down. If, on the other hand, you just know that you've neglected yourself and your needs for far too long, this test will pinpoint precisely those areas that need to change, giving you the breath of fresh air that will set you grinning through even the most challenging of days.

It's important to realise that there are two vital roles that must get some of your attention in life. So often, we find that only one of them gets noticed regularly and it's the other that is forgotten in the humdrum routine of daily life. I'm talking about both the worker and the manager in you. Yes, I know. As if you hadn't already got enough to do! The 'worker' in you is the one who beavers around getting everything done; the 'manager' in you is the one who gets the chance to take a snapshot of your overall life, the one who can detect which areas are holding you back and which areas are propelling you forward. It's extremely easy, especially for us girls, to neglect the manager in us, as the worker is so overwhelmed. The Allen Stress Test will give the manager in you the chance to shine for a second and give you a snapshot from above to see if you like your life.

The Allen Stress Test is split into five sections: Home, Work, Health, Relationships and You. It's up to you to simply tick 'yes', 'no' or 'sometimes' with complete honesty. You may be surprised to discover where you thought your stress spots were and where they actually are. It may be, for instance, that your answers suggest that situations you had considered to be tolerable are the cause of much of your anxiety and stress. If that's the case, you'll be able to deal with things by taking on board the tips in this book in the relevant chapters. The point is, if you have to put up with something, it's probably not doing you a whole lot of good. So here goes. Take a pen, make sure you won't be disturbed for the next few minutes and find out what's really bugging you. You are just 25 questions away from the start of your stress-free life!

Home

Does your heart sink when you walk through the door at home and you're faced with everything you have to do before bedtime?

Yes ☐   No ☐   Sometimes ☐

Are you easily frustrated at home?

Yes ☐   No ☐   Sometimes ☐

Do you forget to pay bills on time?

Yes ☐   No ☐   Sometimes ☐

Are you always hunting for something clean/dry to wear in the morning?

Yes ☐   No ☐   Sometimes ☐

Do arguments erupt easily within your household?

Yes ☐   No ☐   Sometimes ☐

Work

Does thinking about going back to school fill you with dread?

Yes ☐   No ☐   Sometimes ☐

Are you short tempered with your class?

Yes ☐   No ☐   Sometimes ☐

Are you disorganised with your school paperwork?

Yes ☐   No ☐   Sometimes ☐

Do you easily see the negative in situations?

Yes ☐   No ☐   Sometimes ☐

Do you feel antagonistic towards other members of staff?

Yes ☐   No ☐   Sometimes ☐

Health

Are you easily brought to tears?

Yes ☐ No ☐ Sometimes ☐

Do you wake up feeling exhausted?

Yes ☐ No ☐ Sometimes ☐

Do you often pick up colds/viruses/infections?

Yes ☐ No ☐ Sometimes ☐

Is your posture poor?

Yes ☐ No ☐ Sometimes ☐

Do you worry that you won't be able to cope for much longer?

Yes ☐ No ☐ Sometimes ☐

Relationships

Do you and your partner bicker easily?

Yes ☐   No ☐   Sometimes ☐

Do you feel that there is a distinct lack of romance and closeness in your relationship?

Yes ☐   No ☐   Sometimes ☐

Do you worry how your mood is affecting your love life?

Yes ☐   No ☐   Sometimes ☐

Does your partner comment on how irritable and distant you are?

Yes ☐   No ☐   Sometimes ☐

Do you frequently let your partner down?

Yes ☐   No ☐   Sometimes ☐

You

Are you always late for everything?

Yes ☐ No ☐ Sometimes ☐

Do you forget things easily?

Yes ☐ No ☐ Sometimes ☐

Do you get frustrated because you're never able to spend any time on your own?

Yes ☐ No ☐ Sometimes ☐

Do you get annoyed that there's never any time to see friends or go out socially?

Yes ☐ No ☐ Sometimes ☐

Do you get so caught up in the day-to-day things that you forget the big picture about where you want your life to go?

Yes ☐ No ☐ Sometimes ☐

Results

Mostly Yes

You feel out of control in most areas of your life right now but there are probably some that are worse than others, so pay attention to the number of yes answers you have and in which category they are. This will give you an indication of where you need to concentrate your efforts first. This is a valuable exercise, so don't be put off by your score – use it as a basis to change the things that aren't working for you. If you scored worse in the Home section, check out 'Home – Hassle = Smiles from teacher[2]' on page 75. If it's work that's bugging you, you might well find some answers in 'Watching children GROW' and 'Dealing with difficult parents' on pages 51 and 28. If it's your health on the other hand, have a closer look at what you eat with 'Trick or treat?' on page 101 and learn tips about how to relax. If your relationship is taking the strain, take heed from 'Switching off' on page 147 and 'And then she said …' on page 91, or have a look at 'Courting couples' on page 166. Finally, if the main bulk of your yes answers belonged to the You category, then take some time to read 'Self-preservation' on page 82 or 'H is for health' on page 181 and try some of those tips. My main message? You've been working hard; now see if there are any steps you can take to make life easier. It may also be beneficial to read 'Legitimate stress' on page 55. If you're constantly feeling stressed in every area of life, check out this chapter, because it may well help you to feel calmer overall.

Mostly No

You've pretty much got life under control, (this is your cue to smile broadly and feel rather smug, by the way!). If there are a few yes answers sprinkled in there every so often, hey, you're only human – don't get downhearted! Use this book to find a few alternative ways of dealing with the pressures you face and stay focused and positive, because right now you're in a good place, so make sure you stay there.

Mostly Sometimes

This is an ideal time for you to be looking at the habits you've developed. You do sometimes feel stretched in some areas of your life and, although that does have an impact on you, you manage it well and are keeping your head above water – you're still swimming! What you can do by using the tips in this book is to target your weaker areas and turn those into your strongest. Make sure you do some vital groundwork now before stress gets a firmer grip on your life.

Parents' evenings

Ever wished you didn't have to attend yet another parents' evening? Do you struggle to connect with parents who just don't seem interested in their children's education? Perhaps you shy away from confrontation and hate the thought of telling a parent the truth about their little one's abilities and behaviour. If that's you, this is the perfect strategy.

Parents evenings – chore or delight? The teachers I've spoken to have mixed feelings. On the one hand, it's an essential time for one-to-one contact with the parents you never get a chance to see. After all, it's the children you spend most of your time with, and those children probably spend more time with you, their teacher, interacting and learning, than with their own mum, dad or carer. Parents are the faces behind the stories told in the classroom, and it's your chance as their teacher to use these meetings to understand your pupils on a deeper level.

You'll have only a matter of minutes to meet the parents, but you'll subconsciously take in a great deal of information in that short time and, once you've done that, it will lead to a deeper understanding of their child and how you can best help them. It's an opportunity to get to know a child's background and beginnings. Parents' evenings uncover a variety of links between a child's behaviour, attitude in class, ability and concentration levels, and those links give you an insight into the possible reasons behind any problems. As a trained professional, you'll be able to understand why a child is struggling or shy, disruptive or naughty. For instance, you might learn that relations at home possibly aren't what they seem. We all know that children need routine, and school provides that, but, if their home life is disruptive, shaky or unstructured, that will account for a lot.

One teacher I spoke to, Vanessa, was concerned about an eight-year-old in her class. She was shy at the best of times but was retreating further into herself and spending more and more time on her own. When Vanessa asked if everything was OK at home, she said, 'I don't think my daddy lives at home any more.' Of course, when parents' evening came around, it transpired that Daddy did live at home but had a demanding career that meant he spent much of the week on the road. His daughter genuinely thought he didn't live with them any more.

Parent–teacher meetings are a vital part of getting to know your pupils better, understanding where they come from and how each one can be helped. So why is it that the parents' evening has the ability to strike fear into the hearts of even hardened teachers up and down the country? Well, there is another side to this important evening spent talking about little minds, and that's the parents themselves, with their rose-tinted glasses and illusions that their offspring will one day be applying for membership of Mensa!

Any parent naturally wants to hear a glowing report, ten out of ten for effort and remarks such as 'Concentrates hard', 'Has a bright future' and 'Excels in the classroom'. They lean forward desperate to hear that their pride and joy tidies up as the teacher asks, displays immaculate manners at all times and personifies the model pupil. After all, they know that their child's behaviour is a reflection of their own skills as parents. If this isn't the case, the teacher could be in for a rough ride. You know you have to be honest, but facing a disillusioned parent, it seems, is far scarier than standing in front of thirty out-of-control eight-year-olds!

While some parents, of course, are good-mannered, pleasant and keen to understand how to further their child's education, others will be rude, arrogant and completely dismissive of their little darling's disruptive behaviour in class. So how do you cope with telling a parent something they really don't want to hear? How exactly do you break it to a doting mother that her child is actually the class horror and the worst pupil you've seen in your entire teaching career to date? Let me guess: you'd rather stick pins in your eyes, right? Well, with this strategy, hopefully you won't have to go that far! This is my two-step plan.

Step 1: Positive bedside manner

First of all you have to protect your comments. By that, I mean that you start the conversation on the positive side. In short, I like to call it PBM – 'positive bedside manner'. Yes, even teachers need a bedside manner!

Parents want to hear great things about their children – it's only natural – so make sure you have at least two positive things to tell parents about each child. This doesn't need to be time-consuming: you can do it on the way to the parents' evening if you like, while driving, or even while you are washing up a few days in advance. Think of each child for thirty seconds and come up with two positive things to say about them. Write them down if you get the chance, but, even if you don't, the very act of thinking about the positive qualities of each child will leave you with a lovely word of praise at the ready when faced with the parents.

If you do have time and prefer to write it down, the form below might be helpful.

Childs name:_____

I like_____ because_____

_____ is helpful in the classroom

because_____ has grown over the

past year because_____.

This will prepare you. It will be a conversation opener and give the parents something to cling to in even the worst-case scenarios! If you choose to use this form, you could give it to the parents after you've spoken to them, so they can show their child when they get home. I must admit, when I was at school, I never did anything really outrageous, so my school reports were never awful; but waiting for Mum and Dad to walk through the door was agony. When you're sitting at home imagining all sorts of scenarios, it would be really nice to know not only that your teacher likes you but why they like you. Children are just starting to learn about behaviour, qualities, values and who they are, so feeding that information back to them is essential for a child's self-esteem as well as their parents' ego.

Step 2: The GROW Model

Now to the inevitable – the bit the parents won't want to hear – and this is your strategy: the GROW model. This is a common life-coaching strategy that can easily be adapted to all kinds of scenarios and is a great tool to use in a parent–teacher meeting. Here's how it works.

The G stands for *goal*. This is where you are aiming for the child to be. The R stands for *reality*, where the child is at the moment. The O stands for *options* – how you and the parents can work together to help the child to get to the goal. And the W is the *will* – what you have both decided to do to help the child move closer to *their* goal.

This is a straightforward strategy that involves parents in making choices and coming up with different solutions as well. For instance, if a pupil is tired every morning and can't concentrate, one option could be that Mum could make sure he's in bed earlier and that the television is switched off or removed from the bedroom altogether. The teacher could suggest bringing him to the front of the class, so he is closer to her to prevent his attention from wandering. This also helps you to come to the table with a strategy that will make saying difficult things to parents a whole lot easier.

It's the options part that is key here, since it gives parents the opportunity to come up with solutions or strategies to try. It means that they leave the meeting with a plan of action.

Bringing the GROW system to parents' evenings will give it a positive structure that will make stressful conversations easier.

I recommended my two-step plan to Danielle during her first year of teaching. She was nervous about meeting the parents of a little girl who had been behaving badly. She'd met the child's mother briefly before and was not given a warm reception. The last time they had met, Danielle had described the child's behaviour to the mother and told her that she'd been picking on other children, throwing tantrums in the class and was often to be found in tears. Instead of being a concerned parent as Danielle had expected, the child's mother was rude and didn't seem very concerned about her daughter. What was worse, she thought that her behaviour was perfectly normal and told Danielle that she had better things to do that day than be treated like a naughty child herself!

Following my conversation with Danielle and her willingness to take the child's mother through my two-step plan, she opened the conversation differently, this time using the most brilliant, positive bedside manner she could muster, and then followed it with the GROW plan, involving the parent in both the problem and the solution.

The meeting went much more smoothly than Danielle had expected. Later she told me that her new positive bedside manner worked a treat, because the child's mother was immediately calmer. Instead of standing face to face, she had invited the mother to sit down with her and both of those strategies had meant that she felt confident about going through the GROW plan.

The mother confided that her daughter's behaviour was also disruptive at home and she had wondered whether more one-to-one time with her after school might help. The mother agreed to take her daughter out to play every evening directly after school so they could talk about what had happened during the day, and Danielle said that she would give the child a job to do every break time to prevent her from becoming disruptive when she got bored. It's just fantastic to hear that Danielle and the child's mother are now working together and with great success.

Next time a parents' evening comes around, follow Danielle's lead. Swot up on this tip and get the very best from your meeting.

Monkey magic

How on earth do you help a child who isn't coping, when you have to spread your attention among 29 others in the class? The trick? Get them monkeying around with this very useful tool.

When children aren't coping at school, when they're crying for no reason or when it's obvious they're finding it hard to concentrate, there is a strategy that can be taught to the whole class to identify specific problem areas and help guide children into identifying and dealing with new and challenging issues.

Rose was concerned about one of her pupils, Ella. Ever since her best friend had left the school, she had turned from a bright and vivacious child, bordering on the 'overenthusiastic', into a quiet little girl who was losing her confidence with the other children. Rose thought that Ella's lack of confidence was probably due to the fact that her best friend had left the area, but needed to help her identify for herself why she was so unhappy in class and give her something to help her handle the situation better.

Monkey magic really helped in this case. Rose handed out an A4 page with monkeys down the left-hand side, as in the illustration on the next page.

She then described to the class that this was the 'Monkey-on-Your-Back Game'. Monkeys were the things that made you unhappy. These were the problems that you had and, if you wrote them down, you could deal with them one by one.

In short, monkeys are representations of problems, i.e. emotional issues, things that the children aren't coping with very well or don't like. By identifying their monkeys and writing them down, Rose's class took them off their backs and they started to work towards feeling better about situations. The children in Rose's class wrote down worries such as homework, spelling tests and SATs and, yes, one of Ella's was her best friend's departure. It's a way of getting them to start writing down their problems from a young age. This teaches them to deal with them instead of living with them without confronting issues. It teaches them not to carry their monkeys around with them everywhere.

This worked so well for Rose's class that she began to do it as a weekly exercise. Each week, the class has five

Monkey Magic

minutes of Monkey Magic. When children write things down, problems don't always seem so bad and they can talk them through with their parents or teachers.

Dealing with difficult parents

They're out there. You know who they are. But that doesn't make dealing with them any easier. Difficult parents – the bane of your lives. Well, maybe it needn't be so difficult with a little rapport.

Building a rapport, that's the answer. It's simply going to make your lives a little easier, ladies, particularly for those of you who are relatively new to your profession. It's important to build a rapport with parents, even the most difficult ones. If you can build up a relationship with parents, especially the parents of those children who need a little extra attention, it's going to make the next term just that little bit less stressful.

If you approach parents as human beings, they'll be less intimidating and you'll be able to encourage them to take an active part in their child's development. If you explain to parents the processes that their child is going through at school and establish a rapport with them, they'll be more inclined to listen to where you're coming from. Building a rapport quickly with just anyone isn't always easy. Some people are a breeze to get to know and a joy to chat to. They'll open up to you and come across as friendly, kind and easy to talk to. Others, though, find it hard to build relationships with those they see every day, let alone a teacher they see just a couple of times a term. In difficult circumstances, if their child is not performing well or causing a problem in the classroom, it falls to you to be a bit more inventive with your social skills.

Direct eye contact and smiling are, of course, our first impressions that someone likes us, and building a rapport with someone is all about liking and respecting each other. Even with those parents who don't instantly look like the type of people you could get on with, you'd be surprised what you have in common when you start talking to them. Investing a few minutes in asking parents about themselves and what they do, just as other people would in a social situation, helps to open up lines of communication.

During one difficult conversation with a parent of her Year 7 class, Joan needed to tell one family that their son was the cause of bullying in the playground – not something any teacher relishes explaining. At the beginning of their meeting, Joan asked a few questions about the parents and discovered that they owned an MG Midget, as she did. They both had a real passion for old cars and they belonged to the MG Owners' Club, as she did. In fact, they were able to tell her where to find certain replacement parts. The conversation was still a difficult one to tackle but, with the help of a joint passion for classic MGs, a relationship had been struck up and the parents took the news relatively well. They worked together to get to the bottom of the child's behaviour. If you think you are nervous about meeting the parent of a disruptive child, you can bet your bottom dollar that they will be even more nervous about what you're going to say about their son or daughter!

Whatever the event, whoever you're trying to get along with, building a rapport with someone is a skill and it can be very easily learned. I've found that, especially when women try to build up a rapport with other women, the most amazing relationships have been struck by paying a compliment. Imagine for a second that you are the parent and you have to meet a new teacher for a progress report. Imagine how different you'd feel if that teacher gave you a compliment, commented on something you were wearing or carrying, such as a necklace or a handbag. It's actually not often that women tell each other that they think they have great style or love an item of their clothing. Somehow it's just seen as 'too personal' to mention. But it's far from too personal: every woman loves it when someone comments on her style. Now, before you go around lying through your back teeth just to get on side with someone, know this: the compliment has to be genuine! Don't fake it, whatever you do: the recipient will see straight through you and you'll come across as sarcastic, which will do you no favours at all!

It doesn't matter what your profession is – when a genuine compliment is paid, I've seen women physically grow inches taller. It's an instant way to build a rapport and in a difficult parent–teacher scenario it goes some way towards making comments about their children less of a personal attack and more of a search for a solution.

So remember four speedy ways to build rapport: make eye contact, smile warmly, find something in common and, lastly, give a genuine compliment, and you'll make astounding progress, whatever you're doing.

Summer holiday nightmares for mothers

Ah, those precious summer holidays! And now it's finally time for your own children, isn't it?

Don't you just get fed up to the back teeth of people who work in other professions? 'Oh,' they say dreamily, 'lucky you! You get six weeks off every year. What a rest!' Or they'll remark sarcastically, 'You're never at work – you get a holiday every six weeks!' If only they knew.

When summer holidays come round, you're exhausted, you've stretched yourself and your pupils to the very limit to get through end-of-year tests, sports days and school plays and you've probably spent hours working after school to make this all happen. You'll have spent yet more time on school trips than you care to admit, keeping count of little heads bobbing up and down through crowds, and you're probably feeling physically and mentally exhausted.

Even though it's school holidays for pupils (including your own children if you have them), the likelihood is that you'll still have to go into school at some point to catch up on paperwork and prepare ideas and lesson plans for next term. Suddenly, your enviable six-week break starts to look a little less attractive. It is therefore important to make the most of your break and spend some special time with your children. In case it's not possible for you to go away and you can't spend a fortune on theme parks to keep the children amused, here are my top ten tips on how to make those days with your children just as special as you try to make term time with your class.

1. **Become artistic.** Buy a canvas and get the kids painting pictures for their bedrooms. Emulsion tester pots wash off little fingers easily and a weekend paint fest will get creative minds buzzing, bringing out the impressionist in them!

2. **Walk more.** Take the kids on a family walk. If you have a beach near you, that'll be ideal, as the sea breeze will wear them out by the end of the day. If not, look into areas of natural beauty near where you live such as national gardens, forests and parks. These can be great places for families to walk. Buy them pedometers and they'll soon want to clock up the steps. As we all know, exercise is great for using up endless childhood energy, but it also relaxes stressed parents

at the same time. By the time you get home, bedtime will be a breeze, leaving you some well-earned time to yourself.

3. **Keep tempers in check.** You can do this by making sure that everyone's hydrated. Whether you're planning a day out or just hanging around the house making up games with duvet covers and stairwells, make sure that both you and the children drink plenty of water throughout the day. You'll remain calmer and have bags more energy, and the children will be much nicer to be around, since their concentration levels will be vastly improved.

4. **Give yourself a break this summer.** You're allowed one! Refuse to take on all the housework yourself. You don't need me to tell you that bribery goes a long way, so this summer, instead of working yourself into the ground to get the housework done before heading off, already exhausted, to take the kids somewhere nice, bargain with them and get them tidying rooms, feeding guinea pigs and emptying dishwashers first. The payoff? A nicer time out with Mum later on.

5. **Tell stories.** You probably do it at school with other people's children every day and it may even be one of the things you would most love to do with your own

children but never get the time. Take them off somewhere for the afternoon. Find a tree to sit under and make up stories together. This is about relaxation – for you as well as your children.

This is about remembering how to be a child again. You're surrounded by children all day but you're always the one in charge and you can't afford to be a child yourself or else you'd have a revolution on your hands! This is the time for you to remember what it's like to be a child again, how to be inventive by making up stories about fairies, dragons, monsters and castles. Come back down to their level, forget the stresses of last term and laugh by making up silly endings to fairy tales. If you've lost a little imagination over the years, get your children to start off the story.

6. **Teach your children how to massage.** There's no right or wrong way to massage, so you don't have to be a trained therapist to do it. The fact is, massage is one of the most natural ways there is to induce calm and relaxation. Teaching children to massage you gets them learning on all kinds of levels. It encourages them to think of others, teaches them to be considerate and gentle and promotes great bonding between parent and child. Massage makes everyone feel

special, since everyone gets a go. If you're going to get serious about massage, pop to the shops and invest in some lavender or fruity massage oil and get the whole family involved.

7. **Avoid stressful summer holidays.** You can do this by thinking more positively. Thinking and speaking positively works a treat to destress the whole family, from babies to the family dog! Teach your children to refine their language by example. Say nice things about yourself and about them, tell them what they're good at instead of what they're bad at.

Try using the tone of your voice differently. When you're cross with the children, instead of raising your voice, try lowering it, looking directly at them at their eye level and speaking more slowly than normal. I've heard so many fraught parents literally screaming at their children, using swear words and negative sayings in an effort to make them fall in line. Phrases such as 'You're useless' and 'Don't be stupid' trip off the tongue very quickly in tense situations.

During term time, primary school children and their parents have to walk past my house to get to school every morning. I've been absolutely appalled on occasions to hear parents speak to their children – in fact, they aren't so much speaking to them as yelling at them, trying to get them to behave, walk nicely or keep up with them. When parents are stressed, the children feel it and the parents show it; but, by refining your language, thinking about your tone when speaking to a child and quietening your voice when telling them off, you'll be teaching them respect for you and for themselves. Praise yourself and them a lot. You can even turn it into a game by getting them to tell you what they think their own good points are. Get them to write down their strengths for you each day. I bet that'll make good bedtime reading!

8. **Get visualising.** Children have extraordinary imaginations, so spend two minutes conjuring up 'happy places' in their minds. Get them to tell you exactly what they saw and then draw or write about it, so they don't forget. You can do this to music or outside in the fresh air. This is also a fabulous idea for you, too. When was the last time you got stressed and used your 'happy place' to ground you again? Do the exercise with the kids and write down your own happy place, then stick it somewhere you'll see it every day. The inside of the wardrobe door for instance, could remind you of your happy place every morning when you get dressed.

Think about it for just a few seconds while you're getting dressed, and, next time you feel like pulling your hair out, just a couple of seconds in your happy place will remind you that life's not so bad after all!

9. **Mums, say no!** If you get lumbered with everyone else's kids as well as your own, don't be afraid to say no. You're surrounded by noisy, spirited children every day, so do yourself instead of everyone else a favour, and say no to looking after other children this summer. Take the pressure off and enjoy one-to-one time just for you and your family.

10. **Bach Flower Remedies.** These are a must for any parent's cupboard. If you've never heard of them, next time you're in town, take a look in your local health-food shop. There are 38 different remedies to suit all kinds of emotions and Rescue Remedy in particular is great for stressed or upset children and adults. It's great in a crisis to calm the soul. Just a couple of drops on the tongue is invaluable for tired children with tantrums. It soothes frazzled parents, too, and I've even used it on my dogs during thunderstorms or on fireworks night. Its effect is almost instant. The remedies are non-addictive, homoeopathic and easily available in supermarkets as well as health-food shops.

(See their website – the address is on page 214 – for more details.)

Make the time that you have available with your children extra special this summer, and that'll be another area of your life that will feel more complete as a result.

Are you happily pottering?

OK, girls, hands up if you've ever banged a pan or two while tidying up the kitchen, hoping to get someone's attention. Perhaps, on the other hand, you relax by pottering around the house, much to the annoyance of your partner, who feels guilty about not pulling their weight while you're making yourself busy. If you recognise yourself here, then you'll love this new catchphrase. Have you heard of happily pottering? No? By the end of this chapter you'll have adopted it as you favourite catchphrase.

We girls know there is a distinct difference between happily pottering around and quietly steaming as we drop heavy hints to get some attention, while other nameless members of the household sit and do nothing. If we're in one mood, we'll be happily pottering away, tidying, cleaning, mumbling, sorting, throwing away and organising. Then (because we're women) there's the other type of pottering, which will be far from happy – the type where banging doors, hoovering loudly (if indeed one can hoover loudly), sighing heavily, huffing and puffing all prevail.

On days like those, we wander around with a face like thunder, muttering obscenities under our breath, hoping that those, still nameless, members of the household will eventually realise our efforts, get off their lazy backsides and offer some assistance. Of course when/if they do ask, it's our absolute prerogative and birthright to snap, 'I've nearly finished anyway. You carry on watching TV!' We never really mean that, though. What we're actually saying is, 'Yes, get off your behind and help!' Unfortunately though, it's only ever the shrewdest of partners, just a small percentage of the population, who actually under-stand female undertones and move swiftly into action to calm rising tempers.

When Val was being coached, it became clear that, for her, pottering around the house was heaven! It was her way of de-stressing from a hectic school day and she loved that time spent on her own without any interference from anyone. The last thing she wanted was anyone helping and interfering with her 'downtime'. The main problem was that her husband always felt guilty for not pottering with her and assumed that any clangs of crockery in the kitchen were a direct dig at him. She'd be happily fiddling around and he'd be hiding somewhere keeping his head down, thinking he was in deep trouble. This annoyed Val all the more because, for the majority of the time, he wasn't in trouble at all. 'So why does he always expect to be?' she asked quizzically. 'Years of training,' we both agreed!

We had to get Val and her husband to differentiate between 'happy' pottering and 'unhappy' pottering, so we decided to call it 'happily pottering'. Next time Val was bumbling around the house, to clear up any confusion quickly, he'd simply cry out, 'Are you happily pottering?' All she had to do was answer yes or no.

All confusion, you'll be pleased to hear, has now been eradicated. Whether you love housework or loathe it, save time and energy in future and be direct with your family. It'll definitely save on flaring tempers and may even save on the crockery too!

'Tis the season to be jolly, tra-la-la-la-lah la-lah lah lah

Or perhaps you feel like sarcastically screaming, 'Yeah, right, ha-ha-ha-ha-hah ha-hah hah hah!' If the Christmas season for you is one endless round of gruelling rehearsals, choir practices and fraught evenings spent frantically turning those 39 terrors into an angelic semi-professional choir by Christmas Eve, then your own Christmas preparations may get forgotten if you're not totally prepared.

I'm told that music teachers are among the most stressed at Christmas time, and, if you're a music teacher involved with the Christmas production, then you'll know exactly what I'm talking about.

Your days are filled with the challenge of getting the choir together in the same place at the same time, in between their other lessons and activities, meaning that lunch for you in December is virtually non-existent and you spend most of the Yuletide period surviving on coffee and adrenalin. Finally, you collapse in a relieved heap on Christmas Eve once it's all over. Little Johnny *did* remember his solo in the end; tiny Tara *didn't* wet herself through the last act of the play after all, the live donkey (kindly donated by the local farmer) *didn't* run away with the baby Jesus; and the homemade mince pies you knocked up in between rehearsals, wrapping paper and sherry went down a treat with all concerned! Remember the feeling as you sink into an armchair, worn out with a vague smile creeping across your face? But then you sit bolt upright with eyes fixed in that rabbit-caught-in-the-headlamps expression, as you remember your own family! The ones you forgot! If this is you, you'll know that, unless you had the forethought to do your Christmas shopping in August, it's just not going to get done – at least not without a fight!

Ladies, if the secret of organising the whole school and their mothers effortlessly means having to prepare your own Christmas in August, then it's no shame (a) to admit it and (b) to go do it!

Fran is responsible for the Christmas concert at her primary school, and it's been the bane of her life for the past nine years. Every year is the same, as she'd never worked out how to coordinate everything that needed to be done simultaneously both at school and at home. Fran, you see, loves to be involved. She openly admits to biting off more than she can chew with monotonous regularity, and each year it gets just that little bit harder to pull off. Last year, she decided to break the cycle and take a hard look at her routine throughout the autumn term. She listed everything that she takes on and everything for which she agrees to take responsibility. Never one to let the school or her pupils down, she's been known to go to ridiculous lengths to make sure that the Christmas concert is a joy for the whole school but had never really paid much attention to her welfare during this stressful time.

A few years ago, though, Fran made a few changes. Not massive ones, just little tweaks that meant she transformed Christmas for her and her whole family. First, she decided not to invite her family over for Christmas dinner. Instead she asked her parents and brother if they'd mind going out to a pub for the festive meal – not something her family had ever done before. They were reluctant to dine out, but, after she had explained how pressurised she'd been feeling, they agreed to give it a go.

Next, Fran made her Christmas list in August and set about going Christmas shopping on the same day as buying her daughter's new school uniform. An exhausting day of shopping, admittedly, but, even so, Fran still believed it was considerably less stressful than fighting her way through rainy, cold streets on late-night shopping evenings, following hours of out-of-tune carols that continued to twang in her ears after school! Wrapping started in September; cards were written by October and waited, stamped and addressed, ready for posting on 1 December. Everyone commented last year on how much more relaxed she looked, how organised she appeared, and Fran herself enjoyed everything, from the tantrums and tears to the glow on little faces as they sang the last note to rapturous applause.

Don't try to cram everything in, during the month of December. Do yourself a favour this year and get Christmas done early. Whether you're a music teacher or not, being organised for Christmas before you go back to school in September may just make the difference you've been looking for.

Monkey magic for teachers

Feeling overwhelmed by everything you need to do? Do you have a million things on your to-do list and no time or energy to even think about prioritising? Well, you too could get some of those monkeys off your back!

We've already seen how monkeys can help the kids, but have you considered how they may be able to help you as well? Moira used this exercise to great effect to identify what was worrying her. It's an easy way to see what's going on in your life. It's not a to-do list, more of a 'things that are on your mind' list, things that are taking up vital energy space in your head, things that you're worried about and perhaps are putting off doing or don't quite know how to tackle.

Use your monkeys exactly like you taught your class to, in 'Monkey magic' and list five of the most pressing things on your mind at the moment.

Monkey Magic

_____
_____
_____

_____
_____
_____

_____
_____
_____

_____
_____
_____

_____
_____
_____

These don't have to be things associated with work: you might choose to include family issues, relationship or money concerns or just worries about how you're coping at the moment.

Once you've identified your monkeys, use this exercise to take each problem in turn and put a mini-plan together by answering these questions:

If you could do one thing about your monkey to feel better about it today, what would you do?

_____

_____

If you thought about your monkey in a different way, how could you choose to think about it?

_____

_____

Imagine this problem is already solved and ask yourself, 'What action did I take that turned the problem around?'

_____

_____

What you've come up with now are the first steps to being able to deal with your problem effectively. When answering the questions, try to view the problem as objectively as possible, which, means avoiding placing the blame anywhere. At the end of the day, even if the problem isn't your fault, it may be down to you to sort it out, so breathe deeply, take any festering anger out of the situation and, lastly but very importantly, smile while you write down your answers. Hard? I don't doubt that. You probably don't feel like smiling at all; in fact, you probably feel more like bursting into tears than smiling. But by raising a smile, even a small one, you'll be sending feel-good hormones to the brain and you'll find it easier to come up with a solution that will work.

Don't wander around with a whole family of monkeys on your back. Take them off one by one and start dealing with them. You'll literally be walking more upright in minutes!

Watching children GROW

Have you ever felt frustrated with a pupil who has enormous ability but lacks the focus to use it? Perhaps you end up doubting your own skills as a teacher because you just can't seem to get to the bottom of why a child doesn't apply themselves. If so, try using this GROW system on them.

I've spoken to a number of teachers who are incredibly frustrated when they're faced with a bright student who simply chooses not to use their talent for learning and prefers to be the class joker. There are two parts to this tip. The first was inspired by a wonderful teacher called Sally, who decided to turn her language around to see if it made any difference to a little boy in her class. She'd previously spent weeks trying to encourage him to work just that little bit harder, but all to no avail – the message was just not getting through. She decided to scrap the phrases 'work hard' and 'try hard' and replaced them with just one word: 'focus'. She had an inkling that telling the children – and, in particular, this child – to work harder was too general. Did she mean 'listen more', 'talk to your friends less'? Or did she mean 'ignore the notes that are being passed round the room'?

Her choice of words had an amazing effect. She started asking everyone to focus when she wanted their attention and it seemed that it was the focus in the action that brought about the success she was trying to create. For instance, a child can be working as hard as their concentration levels will allow, but if they're concentrating on their writing, when it's the subject *behind* the writing that's the issue, they still won't be taking in the information any more quickly. So Step 1 is to be more specific and ask your class to focus – the chances are they'll focus their attention on you, and then you can explain what you'd like their focus to be on for the lesson.

Step 2 is the GROW system. If you've already read 'Parents' evenings' on page 15, you'll have seen how the GROW system can be used as a useful tool for connecting with parents – but you can also use this tool brilliantly on children.

Older children are able to come up with solutions to problems that we, as adults, perhaps wouldn't have thought of before, solutions that would help them individually. And, as teachers, we may not always have the key to get the best out of a particular child. Sometimes it's about working with that child and asking them to develop solutions to help them focus.

Carey teaches Year 5, and, after being coached to use the GROW system herself, she decided to use it on one particular child, Matthew, who was struggling with French. Matthew generally did very well in most of his subjects, but French was something he just wasn't grasping, and Carey wanted to try something different, something that would help him view French differently, so she talked through the GROW system with him.

As we now know, G is for *goal*, so they decided that the goal would be for him to reach a higher level of under-standing French. R was the *reality*: when they spoke, he was below average. O stands for *options*, so what exactly were his options? Carey asked Matthew what he thought he could do differently to understand French better and to enjoy the class more. He said that he liked listening to stories on tape in English, so maybe he could listen to easy French stories. He said he'd like to try to pick out the words he understood and work up from there. He also said that he would like to practise having more conversations with his big sister in French at home, because she was in the class above him and was quite good. These may seem quite obvious things, but neither Carey nor Matthew's mum had thought of them before. The W, therefore, stands for *will* – what would Matthew decide to try? He asked his mum to track down easy-learning French children's stories on tape and his sister starting saying things in French to him. Within the term, Matthew had caught up with the rest of his class. French is now high on his list of favourite subjects and he even speaks of becoming a French teacher himself one day!

So, stop berating yourself for not being a good enough teacher and take notice of Carey's advice. It's not about working harder for you or the children. Check out your language, be specific with your requests, ask children to focus more and use the GROW system to find out what they think would help them and, you never know, you might just stumble across the next generation of French teachers!

Legitimate stress

Are you becoming stressed over small details that really aren't earth-shattering? Are you starting to turn little problems into huge decisions because you're so wound up? If so, it's time to sit back and work out whether your stress is truly legitimate.

OK – time to admit it. We all become stressed about things that ultimately don't matter. It's easy to do and anyone reading this thinking that they haven't done it is probably just kidding themselves. How many times have we snapped someone's head off for not putting the toothpaste cap on properly? Maybe we've caused a family row because 'someone' spilled half their cornflakes over the worktop again!

I remember how I was reduced to tears one day after a particularly stressful day. The final straw came after I had battled my way around the supermarket and lifted the last bag of heavy shopping into the boot of my car, when the carrier bag gave way and, in slow motion, the six-pint milk carton fell out of the bottom of the bag and hit the edge of the car boot, splitting the plastic container, and the milk spilled everywhere. Seriously, you've no idea just how far six pints of milk can go. Did anyone stop to help? Did anyone come rushing to my aid? You got it: *no*! There I was, standing in the middle of a very busy supermarket car park, international life coach reduced to tears! We all get those days but you know as well as I do that this is the time when you need to sit back and get a grip of your senses.

So what exactly is legitimate stress? Legitimate stress to you might mean something different from what it means to me, but, basically, a legitimate stress is a concern that literally means life or death or at least a massive change in circumstances. I'm talking about the really big stuff that's going to change the course of your life. If a stress is anything other than that, if the truth is that everyone is perfectly safe, well and happy, what difference does it make if the toothpaste tube leaks all over the sink?

This strategy is about adopting an 'Is this going to change the course of my life?' attitude. If the answer is no, then sorry, girls, it's really not likely to be a legitimate stress.

Another question to ask yourself is, 'In ten years, will this really matter?' Again, if the answer is no, then you probably need to take yourself to task. I worked with someone years ago who just never got wound up over the little things. What a wonderful way to breeze through life! Yes, she had her problems and, no, everything didn't always run perfectly for her, but she'd made a decision years before to get stressed only over the things that truly mattered. Just have a think for a second about what exactly stresses you. What's likely to tip you over the edge on the temper scales? What little niggles have the ability to annoy the hell out of you, causing you to turn from reasonably content at 7.30 a.m. to losing the plot by 8.30 a.m.?

Take five minutes to write down the things that you'd start an argument for, go off into a sulk about or things that would simply put you in a bad mood for the rest of the day. List at least five things below. If there are more, feel free to use this time to really get a blast out of your system.

1. _____

2. _____

3. _____

4. _____

5. _____

Next, go through each stress one by one and check if it's a legitimate stress or not. Make sure it's absolutely valid and don't just scream, 'Of course it is!', because I probably won't hear you! If your checklist is anything like mine, you can almost certainly cross 99 per cent of them off right this minute.

By trying to adopt a more relaxed approach to tooth-paste leakages, mud on carpets and fingerprinted windows, you'll save more of your energy to be able to deal with the bigger issues. You'll be far more productive in a day than you ever realised you could be and you're more likely to be completely satisfied with what you've managed to achieve.

I know this is far easier to read than to practise, but give it a go. Worrying over the small things is just a habit that you've chosen (albeit subconsciously) to live by and, yes, raging hormones and rowdy classes aren't going to help. But, next time you're about to blow your top, ask yourself if it's really worth it. If the answer's no, fake a smile, take a deep breath and let it go – go on, give it a whirl!

Windowsill Bay Cocktail List

Are you in need of two weeks on a sunny beach on some unpronounceable island thousands of miles away from home? Would you love the chance to recharge your batteries but know you can't actually leave the country? Take heart and learn how to holiday at home, in style, with the Windowsill Bay Cocktail List.

Now I could say, close your eyes, breathe deeply and visualise white sandy beaches, palm trees dancing gently in the breeze, the warmth of the sun on your tanned skin and the gorgeous Manuel walking towards you with that ice-cold cocktail you ordered. But the disappointment when you open your eyes might just be too much to bear, so read these tips instead for strategies to genuinely lift the spirit – in the absence of Manuel! Time to party, girlies, with my top five Windowsill Bay Cocktails.

Bathroom Breezer

This is where you get to indulge yourself. If you were really on holiday, you may well visit a health spa or treat yourself to a beauty treatment. If your bathroom cabinet is anything like mine, in between the plasters and headaches tablets, there'll be creams, mud packs, face masks, exfoliators, loofahs, body brushes, fake tans, nail polishes, bubble baths – all sorts of things that you buy throughout the year in good faith, believing that you will use them, but, of course, you never find the time.

Treat yourself, by digging them all out, going through them and running yourself a very deep bubble bath. If you've got children, take advantage of grandmothers or workshops for kids and have a holiday in your own bath-room. Within the hour, you could emerge, brushed, exfoli-ated, moisturised and face-packed with skin as smooth as a baby's bottom and smelling like the perfume department at Harrods!

Secret Hotel Relaxer

Now this isn't as seedy as it might sound. My suggestion is pure unadulterated heaven! This is what you do. Get dressed up, put some make-up on and find the best hotel you can. Order your favourite coffee and sit in their lounge area with a very large book! Get completely lost in your book and coffee for at least an hour. When you've finished, you're allowed to carry on with the rest of your day. But for that hour don't think about anything other than what you're reading – and I don't mean read something for work or to do with teaching: find a novel that you've been itching to read and cherish every single moment.

Hilltop Reflection

Taking a holiday is possibly the ideal time to take stock of your life and direction. You may look asleep as you laze on that sun lounger, but your mind is more likely to be buzzing with thoughts of a better, less stressful and more organised life. That 'lazy' time spent with nothing else to do is really a proactive process of thinking how you can take your ideal life from dreamlike state to reality.

If that's you, then there's no reason why you can't have that same reflection at Windowsill Bay. What you'll need to do is take yourself off somewhere quiet and daydream. Just get lost in thought about the big picture: where your life's going, whether you're completely happy, whether you're where you always thought you'd be at this stage of your life. If you need a little inspiration, perhaps take this book with you and answer the questions in the later chapter, 'Big-picture stuff – coaching questions for teachers'. You could go back with a new attitude and a new start, having made some decisions to change the way you deal with things, the way you run your day and the direction you're set in. This reflection time is as much about getting to know yourself as it is about getting to know your future. If you're not feeling one hundred per cent happy with your lot at the moment, ask yourself, 'What would need to change to bring on that feeling of total fulfilment?'

Fantasy Fever

When was the last time you made a list of things you enjoy doing? Well, use your holiday at home time to do exactly that. It's important to be purposeful about time off. If you don't, you'll be washing, ironing and cooking your way through each day with only daytime TV to keep you amused – and, boy, will you feel cheated by the time September comes round again! With no real holiday in sight, you have to be inventive about how you use your time, and starting (in true life-coach style) with a list will get you focused. Use the space below to write down at least ten things you enjoy doing, things that relax you and make you stop thinking about work. There may be family you want to visit, friends you haven't seen for ages or activities you want to do, so write them all down and then start planning when you're going to take action.

1. _____

2. _____

3. _____

4. _____

5. _____

6. _____

7. _____

8. _____

9. _____

10. _____

Sunrise Sizzler

Get up at sunrise and go for a walk. No, I'm not kidding! Getting up really early, when you've nothing to do except enjoy the peace, tranquillity and beauty of the rising sun, is exceptionally inspiring and gives you a zest for the rest of the day. If you live near a beach, sit on it; if you live near a lake, sit by it; if you live near a forest, walk through it. I'm not suggesting you go to remote places on your own. Be sensible and safety-conscious while you're getting all inspirational. Take someone with you, even, but do this.

Sunrise is an incredibly beautiful and serene time of the day. You could use this as space to create some special time with your partner or children. Pack up breakfast and, even if it means driving while it's still dark, find somewhere beautiful and watch the sun rise. You'll feel as if you're on holiday for the rest of the day.

You are what you sleep

Staying up late marking? Too much coffee throughout the day? Worrying about how you're going to fit everything in? Then sleep, or rather the lack of it, could be an issue.

This strategy is to do with learning to recognise your body's natural clock and then going with it instead of fighting it. Some people are morning people, waking up with the lark, bright and ready for action, while other people just won't accept that there is life on Earth before 8 a.m.! They'll be the ones who come alive after nine in the evening while you can't keep your eyes open at that time of night. I'm one of those by the way – one of those who can't keep their eyes open beyond 9 p.m. – but give me 6 a.m. and I'll happily switch the computer on in my office and start tapping away at my emails. I learned long ago that mornings are my most productive time of day. I remember studying for my A-levels at the dining room table, with my first cup of tea, in my dressing gown with the sun streaming in. I learned far more in those two hours before school than I could ever have crammed in after *Coronation Street*!

There are a few tricks to working with your body clock, sleeping better and being more productive as a result:

- Identify your natural body clock.

- Drink less caffeine throughout the day. Yes, I know, it's a bit of an obvious one, but it won't surprise you to know that most of the teachers I've spoken to seem to live on coffee and cola! Choosing chamomile tea, fruity herbal teas or even warm water with lemon will leave you more relaxed, hydrated and energised.

- Change your bed often – there's nothing like clean sheets to make you drift off when you do finally hit the pillow.

- *Don't* bring your paperwork into the bedroom – it's strictly a no-go zone, so put it somewhere else!

- Have a warm bath before bedtime with a few drops of lavender oil in the water.

- Go to sleep at the same time each night and follow the same pre-sleep routine, too.

Following the tips above should get you snoring for Britain, and they're all important, but this strategy is predominantly about the first tip: finding your body clock's natural rhythm. You may already know what time of day your body prefers but, if you don't, how do you find out? It may help to consider the following statements.

If you're a night owl, you'll answer yes to most of these:

- Given the opportunity you'd lie in until lunch time on your day off.
- You comfortably stay awake and alert after 11 p.m.
- Your energy levels peak in the evening; you're a real party lover.
- You enjoy stimulating games or activities in the evening.
- Your household know not to make conversation with you first thing or before your second morning cuppa, because they'll get their head bitten off.
- You're always the designated driver after an evening out, because you know you'll be wide awake and have no problem driving everyone home late at night.

If you're a morning person, you're more likely to say yes to most of these:

- You most enjoy relaxing in the evening, doing some-thing sedentary.

- You couldn't lie in past seven thirty in the morning on your day off, even if your life depended on it.

- Going to a late movie is a waste of time for you, since you're likely to fall asleep halfway through.

- You don't like driving at night because it tires you.

- You find yourself relying on coffee to keep you awake into the evening while you work.

Most people are either one or the other, and, as with chil-dren, adults, too, need a good sleep routine. If you struggle to stay up late, forcing yourself to mark schoolwork because it's the only time you get any real peace and quiet, try switching those late nights for early mornings. Try getting up before the rest of your household and working before they even know morning has broken. If mornings are for you, bank those hours as quality ones and use them wisely. Change your routine to suit your body and stop trying to get your body to swim against the tide. It'll only rebel.

It's easy to try to make your body fit into a specific schedule that suits your family's needs, but they'd much rather live with someone calm, relaxed and in control.

Hilary took this strategy very seriously when she realised she'd been completely ignoring her body's best time of day. Like me, she is also a morning person. She is often awake by 6 a.m. but finds herself lying there trying to go back to sleep for the extra hour, knowing that she'll be up late again catching up. I suggested that she try getting up as soon as her body woke up naturally and use that time productively. She did. For the next two weeks, the first thing she did when she came to every morning was put on the kettle and have a warm shower. In ten minutes, she was wide awake and preparing for the day ahead at her dining room table in her dressing gown! That gave her a whole hour and a half before the rest of her family descended on her, demanding her attention. Hilary is now able to go to bed earlier, which she much prefers, and she feels as though the quality of sleep she now gets is far better than before.

This tip is about helping your body to work more effectively, so think about your natural rhythm and try altering your routine for maximum benefit.

Relax kids

Rowdy classrooms? Disruptive children? Even the nicest classes have their moments. Here's the perfect way to relax kids.

We all know that if the children have been nice at school, you'll have waltzed through the day just that little bit more easily than if you've had to tame the tiny terrors before trying to teach them. This could be the perfect way to ensure that your day is a little less frenetic!

Vanessa is a teacher of a class of very energetic eight-year-olds. She manages to control their behaviour for most of the time and, over the years, has developed a great set of tips for dealing with rising noise levels and disruptive kiddies, but even she has days when nothing seems to work. On occasions she's found herself hoarse from trying to beat the noise, frustrated with not being able to teach the children who actually wanted to learn and feeling ill with headaches as a result of the stress.

Vanessa spoke to me about coming up with different ways of dealing with both her own stresses and her classroom skills. We spoke about her personal situation at length, but I also recommended a company I'd come across called Relax Kids, run by Marneta Viegas. Her whole ethos is based on relaxing children, and her work has proved highly effective both with parents and in schools up and down the country. 'Relax Kids is a gentle and fun way of introducing children to the world of meditation and relaxation, so helping them explore their imaginations and their creative talents,' says Marneta. Through her work, Marneta has found that, when children are given the tools to be able to relax properly and deeply, they become calmer, easier to work with in the classroom and more able to take in new information. In short, they make their teachers' lives easier!

Below are just two of the exercises that Marneta recommends — and I have to say that they are just magical. Try them with your class.

Get the children to lie down on the floor and get comfortable and then ask them to close their eyes while they listen to the sound of your voice gently and slowly reading the following.

Floating like a feather

Close your eyes, be very still and imagine your toes are becoming as light as feathers. They feel as if they're about to float into the air. Let them drift upwards. And now, try to feel as if your legs are as light as feathers. They are no longer big and heavy but soft and light. Let your tummy and chest become light, too.

Enjoy this feeling as your body is slowly getting lighter and lighter. Feel that your arms are as light as possible and let your fingers gently relax and float upwards. Finally, let your head become light. Now your whole body is as light as a pile of feathers. You feel soft and relaxed. Slowly allow your body to float upwards and see how light you can be. The lighter you are, the higher you will float. Stay up in the air for as long as you wish, floating totally free. And now, when you are ready, slowly drift down again back to the ground.

Marneta's exercises have proved that when children are relaxed, their behaviour improves, their concentration levels develop and their interaction with teachers as well as other children matures. This is about helping children to feel totally at one with themselves, peaceful and calm, not only on the outside but also on the inside. It's not about telling them what to do, giving them orders that they'll resist or hit back at. These simple exercises are about fuelling their imaginations and inducing deep calm from within.

The next exercise is slightly different but just as effective at soothing any classroom on the edge of destruction. Once again, get everyone to lie on the floor or rest their heads in their arms on the desk and take three deep breaths, before gently reading the following.

Relaxing on a soft bed

Close your eyes, be very still and imagine that you're lying on your back, on the softest bed in the world. The pillow is so soft and the sheets are made of silk and feel so warm and soft against your body. Very slowly, you feel your legs become more and more relaxed. Your muscles start to relax as you gently sink deeper into the soft bed.

Now, feel your spine starting to open and lengthen. Feel your arms gently sink downwards. Allow your spine to sink gently into the bed. Let your neck and head be free and sink down. Let your legs sink into the softness of the bed. You are lying on such a comfortable bed. It feels so soft and warm. The deeper you relax, the more you gently sink. You feel very calm lying here. In your mind, repeat to yourself, 'I am completely calm. I am completely calm.' Stay in this calm state for as long as you wish.

'These exercises changed the way the children felt about themselves and enabled them to concentrate,' says advanced-skills teacher, Jo. 'Children are better able to recognise and deal with their feelings in a positive way. Listening to the Relax Kids CDs had a huge impact on their ability to view themselves in a positive way. This was reflected in their behaviour and attitude to their work. Thinking about what it's done for me as a teacher, I think the main benefit is that the work creates moments of stillness in an otherwise chaotic life. The affirmations are a really good reminder of one's own value and uniqueness, something adults often forget, especially those of us who, like many teachers, struggle to balance our work and home lives. I love using Relax Kids in short bursts,' she told me. 'It breaks up the rigidity of the curriculum.'

Next time your class need to calm down, take them through the Relax Kids exercises. They'll absolutely love them – and I have a feeling you will, too!

Home – Hassle = Smiles from teacher[2]

Are troubles at home bringing you down in the classroom? How are you meant just to switch off those problems niggling away at the back of your mind? If life is a struggle right now and the classroom just compounds the issue, then it's time to take a moment to gather your thoughts.

We all know we're meant to leave family troubles at home, but, if you've got relationship or money issues, arguments breaking out over the dinner table and tears before breakfast, you won't be the first person who has broken down in tears in the car on the way to work, so here are a few tips on solving troubles at home.

It's really important to get to the bottom of issues at home, and, although you may feel that you're already trying to do that, if calm and solutions are not forthcoming and you're getting more and more angry, then try a different approach. You can try to assess the situation first of all by using these questions and writing the answers as honestly as possible.

75

What – and write this in as succinct a sentence as possible – is the actual root of the problem?

_____

_____

_____

Besides you, does that problem involve anyone else?

_____

If yes, does that other person know it involves them, and how much stress you are under?

_____

If no, then list five things you'd need to tell them, in order for them to see your situation.

_____

_____

_____

_____

_____

If yes, they *do* know, then how do you usually react to your partner (or the other person concerned) when the topic is mentioned? Choose as far as possible from the actions below:

(a)   I cry and can't get my point across.

(b)   I storm off and get moody.

(c)   I shout, desperate to get my point across.

(d)   I talk and talk but we just go round in circles and never find any solutions.

Next, look up which reaction is closest to yours and, the next time the situation comes around, think about this tip and try to take a moment to react differently and see what happens. Ready? OK, take a deep breath and consider these alternative actions.

(a)   If you generally cry when dealing with confrontation, you probably won't even think straight, let alone get your point across effectively. So I advocate taking yourself away from the situation for a short while (no, not for ever – just an hour or so until you've calmed down) and writing down how you feel and your point of view. When you feel you are calm enough, give what you have written to your partner.

Now it is important to follow a few rules when doing this: never swear; never put the other person down; don't get involved in blame; and keep it simple, to the point and as factual as possible. Oh, and one other thing: try not to use capital letters. I know this sounds a bit odd but capital letters are seen as the written equivalent of shouting, so try to avoid them. By all means make sure that person is aware of how you're feeling but without putting any blame anywhere. If it helps, once the person has your missive, leave the room again until they have had a chance to read your thoughts and take in your words. Doing this means that you can calmly put your point across without getting choked up, and it could mean that you can get to the bottom of the issue much more quickly.

(b) This is for you, if your natural reaction is to storm off and get moody. Unfortunately, you of all people probably know that sulking never really got you anywhere. Solutions cannot be found by not talking and they can't be found by spending time in a different room and locking yourself away, so it's time to be very brave and stay put, exactly where you are. Try to make sure that you and the other person are sitting down, because it takes away any impression of aggression in your posture. If your partner isn't sitting down, pull up a chair and gently suggest that you both sit. Now, if you're not used to talking, this isn't going to feel entirely comfortable, but do stick with it. Apart from chairs, you also need one extra piece of kit for this to work effectively: an egg timer! Give each of yourselves just three minutes to put your opinions/feelings across. This forces you to be as straightforward and direct as possible. Again, don't swear, don't shout and try not to apportion blame – this three minutes is to put across a point of view and your feelings. If this is really hard, you could start by using sentences that start, 'I feel …' or 'I am …'.

c)   If you feel that shouting is your only option for getting your point across, I wouldn't be surprise if it sounds as though a war had broken out in your house. It may be that you're the shouter and the other person is more likely to cry – this behaviour is dominating and can be frightening. If your partner is also a shouter, then it'll be a very noisy household! When your temper rises to the point of shouting, take a physical step backwards, stop talking for three seconds (count in your head) and then *whisper* your point – yes, I am serious; no, I'm not joking! Whispering an argument means that people are more likely to be quiet and will have to listen intently to hear your words and, more to the point, look at you. When disagreements erupt, it's important to look at the other person, be it your partner, daughter, son or parent. Take the noise levels right down and you could be surprised with the outcome.

d) If you talk and talk but end up with the same arguments and same lines every time, it'll be frustrating and boring and you'll feel more like a hamster in a wheel than a person trying to find a solution. Tip number one is to move your argument somewhere else, either to another place in the house or outside the home. Walking, for instance, or being in a different coffee shop automatically changes something about your argument and you'll be less likely to come up with the same solutions. The action of walking will clear your head, so try it and see. Tip number two is to ask each other what outcome you both want and then work backwards from the perfect solution. Again, a strategy like that helps you to look at the situation from a different angle. Instead of working towards finding a solution, you're finding the solution first and then working out how you get there amicably.

When you choose to take a different stance in an argument, choose to take your argument somewhere else, alter your body language or the tone of your voice. It can have amazing effects on the other person and can make the difference between getting nowhere fast and moving forward with a solution.

Self-preservation

When was the last time you had a hysterically funny chat or night out with a girlfriend? It isn't selfish. It's called self-preservation and, if you think the only way you're going to relax is by creeping off to the staff loos and chanting 'ohm, ohm, ohm' for five minutes, think again.

When you're in a stressful career such as teaching, you need a release of pressure from time to time. I'm sure you'll have your favourite ways to unwind. You might exercise, take the dog for a walk, spend time with your family or even try to be on your own to reflect and calm down. But what this tip is promoting is plain, simple, old-fashioned fun with the girls.

As family and work commitments grow, it's ridiculously easy to let relationships with girlfriends slide. No woman, however, can live happily without girly chats for very long and if the stress is showing in your life, either on your face or in your temper, then redress the balance and make contact with friends you haven't seen for ages. Making time for adult conversation at a spa or a wine bar, for instance, is a necessary way of letting your hair down and it doesn't need to eat into hours of family time either. If it's planned properly, you can always fit in a quick hour. If your time is limited, as I would imagine it is, a coffee in town will do, as long as you're both away from phones, children and to-do lists!

Support experts Linda Westall and Angela Ward set up their own group for women, Women on Top, for exactly this reason. 'As women,' says Linda, 'we naturally put everyone's needs before our own, often juggling many balls in the air at the same time and we expect "the balancing act" to happen day in and day out no matter what! But what happens when it all gets too much and those balls come crashing down? It all falls apart, and whose fault is that? Ours, of course! Girls, stop right now! It's time to put *you* first for once. Yes, that's right: *you*! No guilty feelings, now – you can do it. Why? Because if you don't feel good about yourself there's no way you can continue the balancing act.'

When you give in and meet up with your girlfriends, you'll feel completely relieved at not having to be responsible for anyone else for an hour or so. You'll also feel lighter at heart, knowing that you have a couple of clear hours to moan with friends who understand exactly where you're coming from. We all know that, when it comes to moaning and sympathising, there really is no alternative to a good girly gossip. Not only does it give you time to vent your frustration but it takes your head out of your own situation for a few minutes and at the same time gives you a chance to look at how everyone does or doesn't cope. It's easy to become introverted about our own problems, workload and dilemmas and hearing about someone else's for a while can only help.

I know that when I meet up with my friends, and regale them with ridiculous stories of what's made me stressed, they usually end up in fits of giggles, and, of course, I usually end up with hysterical tears of laughter rolling down my face about my own stressful situation! Once someone else finds your situation funny, you can start to see the humour in it too. When you talk through the complete scenarios of your problems, they're usually so distressing that they become hysterically funny, especially after a glass or two of vino!

Jennifer took this on board and decided to get the female teachers at her school together for a coffee and a cake at a nearby bar. She requested just an hour of their time. There may be teachers whom you never really get a chance to talk to or others who look so frazzled that you'd be scared to say hello in case they bite your head off. In a situation that takes those ladies out of the workplace, they're likely to turn back into normal women with a sense of humour. Jennifer's colleagues decided to make this at least a termly event – that, granted, is not very often – but, if you can release some tension, even once every six weeks, you'll be far better equipped to deal with everything else as well.

Linda Westall says that it's so important to talk to your colleagues and girlfriends, because they often have the same juggling act to perform as you and feel that they, too, are always at the bottom of the list. Finding 'me' time is not easy, but doing it with someone else makes it all the more enjoyable. Sharing with other women your worries and concerns about family, health or work lifts your spirits. Females have a great knack of being able to open up to each other much more easily than men. It's a gift, so use it! Get that feel-good factor by sharing your troubles, your dreams and success over a cappuccino and end it with a girlie hug and you'll find yourself on top of the world, ready to juggle the balls again standing on your head!

That release is so badly needed and you may not realise how important it was until the next day. That's when you'll feel your energy levels have increased and you'll be buzzing with enthusiasm and suddenly you'll have a whole new relationship with your colleagues – that is, if you didn't go too mad on the vino!

I is for investing

Feeling completely sapped of energy and enthusiasm? Is it becoming hard to tell when one day ends and another begins? Then use today to think outside the box.

Don't worry: investing in you has nothing to do with bank accounts or interest rates. I'm talking about stimulating your mind, developing your interests and learning something just for you – something that has absolutely nothing to do with being a teacher. I'm talking about getting your mind stimulated in some other way without even the slightest hint of marking.

Would you like to learn something new? When was the last time you considered educating yourself more? And, yes, I do know what you're thinking: that you're exhausted enough as it is now, without another teacher imposing timescales, homework and a pressure to excel. Far from making you wilt, though, investing in you will do completely the opposite – it'll help you to feel refreshed, invigorated and alive.

Education is in you but you spend so much time educating others that, if you're not careful, your own mind will become overloaded with pressure, responsibility and the seriousness of the school system. I'm not talking about exams or long-term qualifications. Instead, there are hundreds of one-day workshops around in the summer holidays and at weekends, allowing you to take time out of your usual routine and to try something new for yourself. There are complementary therapies such as reiki, yoga, Indian head massage and reflexology. These are hugely valuable ways of destressing, but also innovative ways of connecting with loved ones. So investing a day or two in studying at a summer school near you will bring added rewards when you return to school with a brand new recipe for success – and you might be able to use your new skill to teach your class something different. In any case, it will give you space to distance yourself from your career for a while and do something for yourself.

If that doesn't float your boat, then how about pottery classes, wine tasting, chess or riding? All of these activities will need a certain amount of concentration but you'll be using your brain in a different way, which will leave the part you use all the time free to have a rest for a while.

India is a teacher of Year 5 pupils. She has a toddler herself, so she's surrounded by children all the time. Her husband works long hours, which means that by the time he gets home she's beyond exhaustion and can barely string a sentence together. As well as becoming tearful with frustration and tiredness, she found that her once beloved career was turning into a nightmare scenario 'It really wasn't meant to be like this,' she told me, so we decided to use one evening a week to invest in her. Like that of most teachers, her workload was mammoth and India hadn't been taking so much as a second to look at her situation from a different angle – there had been no time! Coaching was her chance to take a few moments to see her life as it was – an endless round of school and work with the added responsibility of feeling like a single parent in the evenings because of her husband's demanding job.

The last thing India wanted to do after a difficult day was to get dressed up and go to a class. There's no doubt it took some persuasion to get her to look up some courses that might interest her. She saw one evening course for beginners in interior design, and in her pre-teacher-training days she'd quite fancied that, but teaching had taken preference. This wasn't a heavy course – just eight weeks, one evening a week – and it was local. She asked her husband if he could make sure that he was home early enough to take care of their daughter on course nights and, knowing she had that assurance, she signed herself up. I spoke to her one month into her course and she was loving it. There was virtually no homework and it didn't require a huge commitment, but it gave her an interest that was totally different to work. She'd made some lovely friends and agreed that she still had lots of energy and felt more positive the following day. The old saying, 'A change is as good as a rest', seems to be true. When we alter our routine and use our brains in a different way, it can make a tremendous difference to how we think and feel about the rest of the week.

If you could do something different just for fun for a couple of hours a week, what would you like to do? Allow yourself the very best and you'll be able to give the very best of yourself right back again.

'And then she said ...'

Do you find yourself going on and on about work, even when you're meant to be enjoying family time? Then this is how to switch off.

Perhaps you don't even know you're doing it, but has anyone in your family ever sighed as you mention for the millionth time the conversation you had with Mrs So-and-so? Well, if so, this tip is probably more for your partner than you!

When things aren't going well, it's natural to go over and over events, situations and conversation in your head. Yes I said *natural* but don't conflate that with *healthy*. There are two things that happen when you do this.

1. You go over it so much that you get more and more upset about the situation, wind yourself up to the point of exhaustion and end up going around in circles with no way out.

2. You'll go over and over it until your family reach screaming pitch and you'll end up arguing with them. You'll *still* have no answers and, as far as your family

are concerned, you'll probably scrap every solution they come up with, which will mean that pretty soon they're going to stop trying, which isolates you even more. In short, they'll get fed up of trying to help. Is this starting to sound familiar?

There are a couple of things you can do to resolve this situation though – starting today.

First of all, you need an off switch. Remember, I did say this is mainly for your family and not you! Your off switch is situated on your upper arm. Yes, it's invisible to the naked eye and, no, I'm not losing my marbles. This is how it works. Whenever you've gone on too much about a certain subject you have to give permission to your loved ones to control your off switch! It means they've had enough, girls!

With the best will in the world, there's only so much they'll be able to take before they're bored, frustrated on your behalf and unable to help you any further – and you'll be eating into valuable time meant to be spent with your family, not just in body but in spirit as well. People feel valued not only when they have you there in person but when you're there in mind, too, and it's massively important for them that you switch off from work. It'll do you untold favours at the same time – trust me! Romantic dates are just not romantic if you're going on and on about your headmistress all evening; and your friends will have only a certain amount of patience, too, before they become bored with your problems and stop listening.

When people stop listening and start making comments about your being there in the physical sense only, you'll feel even worse and it'll make them want to avoid you. Either way, it's not helpful for anyone and can badly damage relationships.

Once they've hit the off switch, what do you do? After all, part of the way we process the information needed to solve problems is to mull it over in our minds, and, if you can't burden your family with that, how on earth are you going to find the answers? Your solution is to find someone specific to speak to, someone you trust who will listen confidentially – in other words, a mentor. Your mentor needs to be someone you can talk to easily for a set period of time, say an hour. It can be someone at school or a friend who's completely out of the school circle, whoever you feel is more appropriate.

What you're asking from them is space in which to go through everything in your head, without asking their advice (you won't take it anyway). Ask someone if it's OK if you nominate them as your mentor and agree to meet up. Tell them that you're just after an ear and that they really don't need to say anything at all. It protects family relation- ships and close friendships from the drama of 'I told you so' and stops resentment from building up as your problems encroach on their special time with you. Time spent with your children and your family should be exactly that: doing things with them, chatting about general things. But, as soon as you realise you're going into 'moan mode', check yourself before they reach for your off switch. With a little practice you could even find yourself looking for your own switch!

I don't mean that you can't ever tell your partner about your worries, but what I am saying is that there is a differ- ence between letting them in on your life and letting the problems be your only form of conversation.

If there isn't anyone who springs to mind who might agree to mentor you, then you could think about a life coach or a counsellor. There is a difference, by the way – we are a breed apart. Don't panic that I'm mentioning a counsellor. Counsellors are just people who are specially trained to help others cope with difficult situations. They are very good at listening and being impartial, and are skilled at helping you to sort things out and to look at the reasons behind your feelings. They have no motive other than your welfare and there is no shame in employing their services. You'd be surprised at the number of people who do – it's just that they don't go telling everyone, and indeed there's no reason why they should.

On the other hand, a life coach can help, too. They'll ask you questions during sessions that help you arrive at your own solutions. They don't tell you what to do and they certainly don't make any decisions for you. They allow you to create your own wonderful solutions that will work in with your lifestyle and with your identity and personality.

A client of mine, Jo, says that having a life coach, 'means that you have a planned release'. She saves up everything to tell me throughout the month, which means that her stresses don't get in the way of her relationships and she doesn't burden others at inappropriate times.

If you want to try using this tip in your life, then you'll need to do two things: (1) tell your family about your off switch and give them permission to use it when you start going on; and then (2) find yourself a mentor and talk everything through with them. You'll feel the weight lift from your shoulders and you'll be able to tackle another day just that little bit better.

Ask Fred

Does it break your heart when kids say negative things about themselves or their friends? Perhaps you understand the damaging effect their words have on their potential to excel but find it hard to explain this to them. Well, maybe it will help to introduce them to Fred.

The subconscious mind and how it works is always a feature of any coaching session I have with a client and any book or article I write. This is because I believe that it is such an important subject and one that people should be aware of. Whether you're being introduced to the idea of the subconscious mind for the first time, or whether you've read about it a thousand times before, it never hurts to bring it to the forefront again, so here goes.

The subconscious is a part of the mind that, as yet, we know fairly little about. The conscious mind is the part of the mind that does all our thinking for us: it makes our decisions and it understands the difference between right and wrong. But the subconscious mind is totally different. It collects information that it hears or sees or otherwise senses, or material that the conscious mind thinks, and stores it, all without ever being able to differentiate between fiction and reality. Consequently, if you tell yourself often enough that you're, let's say, not very good at directions, then guess what! That piece of information gets stored in your subconscious mind as a *fact* – regardless of whether it's actually true or not. Now, fooling yourself into thinking that you're not the world's greatest map reader probably isn't going to cripple your career chances or self-confidence too much for the future, unless you want to be a pilot or taxi driver of course! But just imagine what damage a simple negative thought in a child's mind will do – a thought such as 'I'm not very confident.' Perhaps it's something they've overheard mum or even their teacher saying about them.

As you'll know, primary school is where children start to develop a sense of the kind of person they are, and they do that based on what they hear. I'm quite sure that most teachers reading this are well aware of the effect that negativity can have on a child's development and confidence, but kids can be cruel to each other. Little remarks from other children such as 'You smell' or 'You're stupid' are powerful enough to hurt, and that's where Fred comes in.

By personalising the subconscious mind and giving him (or her) a name – Fred – children are able to understand the subconscious and become more aware of the negative things that Fred listens to and says when they are thinking their own thoughts. Teachers can play a vital role in making children much more aware of the hurtful comments that Fred makes to them and the upsetting remarks that Fred remembers – and there is a game you can play with them.

For older children

Make sure everyone has pens and paper and get them to write down the negative things that Fred (i.e. their own thoughts) says to them. It might be that Fred says they have no friends, or that they can't read well enough or that their sibling is the favourite. These will all be the things that children say to themselves a lot that make them feel down and sad.

Then, next to each negative thing that Fred says, get them to write down the positive alternatives that Fred *should* be saying to them. You, as their teacher, can even make a whole display in the classroom or reception area out of the positive things that Fred says. It will help children to identify the negative things that go through their minds and will also help them understand what happens to other people's Freds when they say something nasty.

For younger children

If the children in your class aren't quite old enough to articulate what they mean or can't as yet write well, they can still do this exercise, because they can draw Fred's face. For instance, if Fred says something negative to them, they may draw a face with a sad expression. On the other hand, get them to draw his face when he says something positive and, with any luck, you'll get a bright, smiley and happy face.

The point of the exercise is to educate children early on about their subconscious minds in a way that they'll understand and appreciate. After the exercise, ask them to be careful what they say to each other's Fred, so their Fred keeps smiling and never frowns. It's a fantastic way of making them more aware of their own language both internally in the form of their self-image and what they say to each other.

Now, while we're on the subject of Fred, what kind of shape is your Fred in? Yep, this is just as important for you as it is for your class. What do you say to yourself that could damage your faith in yourself as a teacher? What do you say to remind yourself that you're too busy, a dreadful organiser or an impatient person? If you're smiling now, it's because you know you could be doing more to make Fred happy too! Make a decision to speak well of yourself. You've taken on an extremely important role as a teacher and your class will learn how to think about themselves partly from how you refer to yourself. Children are perceptive and will pick up on feelings long before they can put words to those feelings, so tell yourself that you're capable, organised and patient and they'll see that confidence in you. It'll ooze from every pore. You just have to believe it first.

Trick or treat?

Do you find that your class run rings around you after a break time spent munching crisps and chocolate? Does what the children consume each break time concern you? Perhaps it's you who's reaching for the chocolate for an instant energy lift. If you're worried that either your diet or that of your class during school break time is unhealthy, have a read of this.

I'm no Jamie Oliver and I'm certainly not after Dr Gillian's job, but because my background is in complementary health, I have a 'thing' about trying to eat the right kind of foods and another 'thing' about trying to cut down on sugar. Since my complementary-health days, I've always been aware that huge sugar hits for children and adults can cause problems in all kinds of areas. Concentration levels fall, bad behaviour ensues and tempers fray – and those are just a *few* of the symptoms, and that's just the adults!

Sugar comes in all kinds of forms. The obvious ones are sweets, chocolate, cakes and biscuits, but there are hidden sugars to beware of in breakfast cereals, tinned foods, microwave meals and fizzy drinks such as colas and lemonades.

Sugar gives the body a very quick burst of energy. It makes the blood sugar level soar and our bodies have to work really hard to bring it down to a safe level. Constantly running your body on very high sugar levels is unhealthy and, when it can't use excess sugar, it will end up being stored as fats – yes, in your thighs!

We all love treats every now and then but don't be fooled by the so-called healthier option. Even the croissants with half an apricot in the middle are still loaded with sugar and are no more healthy than eating a bowl of the white stuff on its own.

Your diet, as a teacher, needs to be one that sustains you through your ludicrously busy day and keeps your energy levels and blood sugar levels steady. We'll come to the good stuff in a minute, but before that I want to tell you about Liz, a qualified kinesiologist, who has put her own Jamie Oliver style of spin on her child's primary school.

Liz's work as a kinesiologist means that she regularly advises people on their diet, and she has a qualification in nutrition to back that up. She is also a normal working mum who takes her child into class in the morning to get him settled. As part of that routine, the mums are encouraged to put their children's mid-morning munchies in their drawers for later, and Liz was very concerned about the types of snacks the other children were having, which included sugary drinks, chewy sticky sweets and bags of crisps. In fact, she was so concerned that she spoke to her child's teacher and asked if she'd be allowed to come in and run some lessons on healthy eating that very young children would be able to understand. The exercises she gave her child's class were inspiring and the children's behaviour after break time on that very first day was a shocking eye opener for Liz, so much so that she called a meeting with the head and has instigated major changes within the school. From the start of the next school year, the children were no longer allowed to bring unhealthy snacks or junk food to school.

Liz has given me permission to share her exercise with you and I'm sure you'll agree that it's an amazingly effective way of getting young children to understand basic nutrition, so feel free, if you think it appropriate in your school, to mirror these classes and see what happens.

Liz brought into the classroom a whole bag of plastic food from her children's play cupboard together with some paper plates. There was a mixture of carrots, meat, potatoes, cakes and chocolate bars. First of all, she picked up each plastic item and got the class to name it and decide whether it was a healthy or unhealthy food. She explained which foods contained the basics, e.g. protein, carbohydrate, fats, and then told them what balance of those things made up a healthy meal. She then asked the children to collect a paper plate and put together their own dinner. Most of the children put together some meat, some vegetables and some starchy food, e.g. potatoes or pasta. What Liz saw next was amazing: most of the better-behaved pupils in the class put together the right balance of food on their plates; the pupils who had found it difficult to sit still and concentrate piled the cakes and sweets onto their plates.

That first day most of Liz's class were listening intently, joining in and in generally behaving well. All hands went up enthusiastically when she asked questions. However, following a break time of unhealthy snack foods, she could barely control the class. The teacher told Liz that this was a regular occurrence. The sugar hits that the children were being given was causing a complete breakdown in their ability to function properly. This isn't only unfair for the children, but it's also an awful situation for you as a teacher, and I can only imagine how high your stress levels soar at this point each day – and they'll continue to soar unless something is done about it. The government has now brought in plans to have healthy school meals as standard, which is an excellent step, not only for the children but also for their long-suffering teachers. In the meantime, however, the above exercise may well benefit you and your class.

Below is a list of healthy foods and suggested breakfasts from Liz. Do take heed when buying breakfast for your own children, when rushing out of the door yourself and when talking to parents or children about their diet – this is important stuff. 'You send your child to school to learn in the right uniform, with the right materials and the right books, but they can't learn properly unless their blood sugar level is stable and their brain is developing properly,' says Liz.

Suggested healthy snacks

- fruit such as bananas, apples, satsumas and grapes, but also try mango or pineapple slices too
- dried fruit – raisins, apricots, prunes and pineapple
- seeds – sesame, pumpkin
- nuts – try brazil, almonds and cashew

- vegetable sticks – try red pepper, carrot and cucumber
- tomatoes, sugar snap peas and celery
- rice cakes
- slices of cheese
- hard-boiled eggs
- ham slices or quiche slices
- vegetable crisps
- make an extra sandwich with wholemeal bread when preparing the packed lunch

Suggested healthy breakfasts for teachers and children

- wholemeal toast and eggs
- wholegrain cereals
- fruit
- natural 'live' yoghurt
- homemade porridge made from scratch (not the microwavable version)
- go continental and offer them ham and cheese!

The long and short of this is that you won't be doing your-self any favours when you next slip out at lunchtime for a quick 'treat'. Just think about what exactly it is that you're 'treating' your body to. A sugar hit making it work overtime to bring your blood sugar levels down safely? An energy rush that'll leave you tired, tearful and exhausted in a matter of minutes?

If it's your children's diets we're talking about, then you'll be telling them off for being naughty and rewarding them for good behaviour with sweets! It's a vicious circle and the key to breaking it is here.

As a teacher, you'll have little enough time some days to draw breath without remembering to eat healthily as well. It's hard enough getting out of the door in the morning, so packing up suitably healthy options to munch on will be the last thing on your mind. We've all done it. You're desper-ately hungry and if the only thing on offer is chips or choco-late, you'll go for it! However, here are my top tips for fast healthy eating that's a genuine treat.

1. Home-made vegetable soup takes a matter of minutes to chop up whatever vegetables you have in the fridge and boil them with a stock cube. Make too much on purpose and freeze small portions. Grab a frozen

portion before you walk out of the door and heat it up at lunchtime.

2. As you unpack the shopping, just give your fresh vegetables – carrots, peppers, celery for instance – a rinse so that, again, on your way out of the door, you can grab some raw veg and eat them at break while on the go if you need to. There's no shame in munching on a whole red pepper, you know!

3. Swap cola and sugary drinks for peppermint tea, water, hot water with a slice of lemon or even beverages such as Barley Cup and Nocaf, which taste similar to coffee but don't have the caffeine.

My favourite tip, which I also practise, is to wash out an empty coffee jar, fill it with raisins, sunflower seeds and pumpkin seeds and keep it in the car. That way, you'll never be far from a healthy snack and you won't be tempted to stop at petrol stations to buy chocolate. Of course, this does have its downside, especially when I stop at traffic lights and am spotted swigging straight from a coffee jar! I have had some odd looks when people must have thought I'd gone beyond stress and taken to eating the neat granules straight from the jar for a more direct and speedy caffeine hit!

If the children are better behaved after eating sensibly, your day will be less fractious. However, even if they're not being angels, if your sugar and energy levels are controlled, you'll be much better equipped to deal with whatever the little darlings throw at you!

List below five things you're going to do differently where your diet is concerned and then make a pact with yourself to try this for two weeks and feel the difference. Over to you!

1. _____

2. _____

3. _____

4. _____

5. _____

Big-picture stuff – coaching questions for teachers

Do you ever feel as if life is just a merry-go-round of events that you slog yourself into the ground for? Do you ever feel as if you never have time to look up and see the bigger picture? These questions are just fantastic!

Big-picture stuff is important. It's the kind of thing we don't get the chance to think about every day. We're all far too wrapped up in what we need to do for most of the time, that tomorrow just seems to appear before you know it, and you've got to start all over again. The big-picture stuff is important if you're to feel as if you have a plan.

This exercise won't take long but it does require you to be on your own and it does require a little attention. You can use this exercise exactly as you wish. You can either close your eyes and pin the tail on the donkey so to speak and just answer the question that you've pointed to, or you can work through each question and ponder it while in the shower. Whichever you choose, do think about it and, if you feel the need, write down a few of your thoughts. You could even keep a bit of a journal if you think it would suit your lifestyle and preference. Ready? As usual take a deep breath and take a look into the future.

- What do you want to have achieved in ten years' time?

- What decisions or problems are you worrying about at the moment and how could you deal with them better?

- What does your most successful day look like?

- What does the future of your dreams contain?

- Which skill do you have that you are most proud of?

- How are you limiting your success?

- How do you love yourself?

- What one thing would make you a happier person?

- What would you regret not doing when you are old?

- Who in your life fills you with optimism and how do they do that?

- What did you learn today?

- Who is the most negative person in your life and how can you deal with that person better?

- What emotional gifts do you give to those who know you?

- What could you do every day to remind yourself how capable you are?

- How would you teach differently if you knew you were the best teacher you could be?

- What would you do differently if you knew you were the best partner you could be?

- How would you act differently if you knew you were the best mother you could be?

- What does 'being free' mean to you?

- What message would you most like to leave behind?

- What does teaching mean to you?

- What does being an inspiration mean to you?

These questions are all meant to be a bit thought-provoking, but they're not meant to fry your brain, so don't spend days worrying about them. Instead, just come up with a few things that spring to mind instantly, mull them over a bit and then think about something else. While you're thinking about something else, your subconscious will be going to work processing the information you've just given it and the information it processes could be useful to you in the future.

The responses provided by your subconscious will give you an insight that perhaps you didn't realise was within you, or it may even confirm a few things that you already knew about yourself. It may even be that, while you were answering your big-picture question, a solution popped into your head from nowhere about how to deal with an issue you have. It's common for answers to come to us when we least expect them, so don't be surprised if this happens. Either way, use this time to think about the bigger picture and take the stress out of the here and now.

Hey, where did my life go?

Were you so full of enthusiasm when you first started teaching that you made a rod for your own back? Have you looked up recently to find you've very little life outside work and want it back again? You're not alone, so consider this strategy.

'Start as you mean to go on.' Isn't that the advice we all repeat to others when entering a new partnership or job? It's all too easy to be so filled with positive energy when you start a new term, new school or even your brand new job as a qualified teacher, that you put your heart and soul into it 110 per cent, with all the gusto you can muster, only to find that you don't actually do anything else except work. While writing this book, I've spoken to several teachers who often wondered whether this could have been the reason behind the breakdown of their marriages. A sobering thought!

One of the most common pressures I've found through my research is that teaching is so demanding that it will take up all of your time if you let it. It's like spending money, I suppose: most of us spend as much as we earn. And it's entirely possible to spend all your time on teaching, marking, after-school activities and meetings and neglect other important areas such as relationships, fun, health, exercise and relaxation.

These are all vital if you are to feel happy and well rounded and you are going to need a regular dose of all of those things. Teaching is one of the most rewarding careers there are, yet, if you think the satisfaction from teaching alone will fulfil you, you've got another think coming. It won't! You'll need more of a focus on you and you'll need more of a focus on those around you, or you could find yourself alone. In short, a fair work–home balance is central and this is how to get it.

Current evaluation

Oh, boy! This is probably the bit you'll want to skip! When you take a look at the reality, it does have a habit of hitting you where it hurts! This is where I'd like you to put your current actions on the timetable below. This is purely an after-school-hours timetable for Monday to Friday, but I'd like you to see exactly where you tend to spend your time.

	4–5 p.m.	5–6 p.m.	6–7 p.m.	7–8 p.m.	8–9 p.m.	9–10 p.m.	10–11 p.m.
Monday							
Tuesday							
Wednesday							
Thursday							
Friday							

Now, if you've filled this in as truthfully as possible, and found that the large majority of your time is spent on schoolwork, your heart has probably sunk to the bottom of your boots. And, if your working day goes on longer into the night than 11 p.m., you probably wondered why my timetable doesn't continue to 1 a.m. Was it a printing error? Doesn't everyone work through the night? No, they don't! And, if you've just cunningly added another column to give you more time, *take it away again*! OK, so you might be a night owl but, crikey, even night owls need some sleep. Whatever you've got to do, try to get it done before 11 p.m. and then give yourself some time to wind down before you go to bed. You may also have wondered why this timetable doesn't include Saturdays and Sundays. It was deliberate, ladies! For all my clients and the teachers I've spoken to, the weekends get swallowed up with things that need to be done. It's just life. You'll be shopping, washing, cleaning and hoovering as well as visiting relatives and cooking for visitors – simultaneously! The weekends, it seems, are the worst time to find time for yourself, so, if you can organise your after-school time more efficiently, it'll be those evenings that will give you the much-needed 'you' time you're craving and the balance between the *work* you and the *personal* you.

The whole reason for this exercise is to help you to schedule some time for other areas of your life, because consistently working into the early hours will simply make you miserable and irritable. Your classes are sectioned into time slots, so I'd like you to use this exercise to divide up your own life outside the classroom in the same way and make sure that you always keep a portion of your time for the things you love doing.

List below five areas of your life that you'd love to spend an hour on each week. It could be talking with friends; it could be special time with your partner or your children; it could be time on your own; it could be time spent on a hobby or even time just spent on the sofa watching soaps (no, it's not a crime, and, yes, even we life coaches are a bit partial to that on occasions!). Soaps aren't the most productive way of spending your time, but, in short doses, they are an excellent way of switching off from the stress of your own life for half an hour and giving your poor grey matter a rest. So which five things would you ideally love to spend an hour doing?

1. _____

2. _____

3. _____

4. _____

5. _____

Excuses? Yep, there are bound to be more than I can come up with, so I'm going to save you the trouble: scrap all of them. If you're prepared to scrap your excuses and rethink your schedule, you'll make huge progress in the getting-a-life stakes. We're going to look at ways in which you can be more productive with your time in the chapters 'Marking among the mess!', 'You work where?' and 'Organising your paperwork to within an inch of its life!'. For now, though, I'd like you to make a pact to shelve any excuses you're preparing and schedule your five new desires into the new timetable on the next page. Use it to schedule your work and your off time and make your life work for you.

Time to focus

When you have your work scheduled, be prepared to concentrate on it and give it your best shot. When you're spending time with your partner or children or on your hobby, be there emotionally and give them – or it – every ounce of your attention. There's nothing worse than saying

	4–5 p.m.	5–6 p.m.	6–7 p.m.	7–8 p.m.	8–9 p.m.	9–10 p.m.	10–11 p.m.
Monday							
Tuesday							
Wednesday							
Thursday							
Friday							

you're going to spend quality time with your partner and then to keep checking the clock so you can get back to your work again. They really won't thank you for it. What do you need to do to focus completely on the task in hand? Turn your mobile off? Take the clock away? Take your watch off? Set your kitchen timer or an alarm, if you wish, to let you know when your time is up. Do what it takes to focus, and trust that you'll have plenty of energy and time left for your work. And follow your schedule.

Try working with your new timetable for a few weeks. Make a real effort to put away your work and spend some time on other activities for a change.

Marking among the mess!

Are you absolutely focused when you do your marking? Do you spend hours doing a job that should take minutes? There's no doubt that the volume of work you have is great, but are you great at being productive?

It's all very well marking for hours on end and spending days planning lessons, but do you really need to spend that long doing it? And are you making the most of your time? If you think the answer is no, then follow my four-step plan for focusing on your work, and you could find yourself speeding through it at a rate of knots.

Step 1: Tidy up

Step 2: Throw away

Step 3: Keep the focus

Step 4: Prioritise

Step 1: Tidy up

Don't expect to feel productive and happy working in chaos. You won't. Even those clients of mine who hate tidying up with a passion still admit to feeling lighter, happier and calmer in an ordered environment. If you just can't see the wood for the trees on your desk, you need to focus on tidying up. The best way to do this, to avoid unproductive hours of moving things around and looking busy, is to clear it totally before you do anything. Take everything off and put it on the floor. Now get the duster out and give it a good clean, and then put back on your desk only what you want to keep on it.

If you come across things you'd forgotten you had, the chances are you don't need them. If it's a piece of paper relating to a meeting that's been and gone and has been actioned, you probably don't need that, either. Any books that belong to other people, put in a pile next to the door to be returned, and any pieces of paper that are related to jobs that you still need to do, put in a tidy pile to create an in-tray. As for numerous pens and pencils, take just a few pencils and a few pens and give the others away. I've decluttered desks before and found money, old photos, children's toys and even laundry! Those things don't belong on your desk or in your workspace; they'll simply make you feel as if you're drowning under clutter. If it helps, use the form below to write out exactly what's on your desk and where it's going to go.

Item on desk	Where it's now going

Try to resist the urge to write 'back on the desk' in the 'Where it's now going' column – it's not big and it's not clever!

Step 2: Throw away

I've decluttered many a client's office before and throwing things away is by far the hardest part for most people to do. If you can answer no to the two questions below – don't even think about it – throw it in the bin, give it away or recycle it. But do not keep it.

- Did you know you had this?
- Have you needed this in the past year?

These two questions will help you make difficult decisions. You're going to have to be firm with yourself. What you're aiming for, is clear space to work in and a proper in-tray for your workload.

Step 3: Keep the focus

When you're working, it's really important to keep your concentration levels up. You simply won't be able to focus properly with poor concentration. Eating the right foods and drinking plenty of fresh water are excellent methods, *but*, if you're still the type of person whose concentration chooses to wander off in the middle of something, you might need another reminder and you might find it helpful to answer this question.

If you were the type of person who found it easy to concentrate, what would you be doing differently?

_____

_____

Many of my clients have answered that question during their coaching sessions and many have come up with similar answers. A popular answer is to have a firmly worded sign that stares them in the face when they look up from their desk. It's a really good way of digging yourself in the ribs when no one's there to do it for you.

I've had clients who've written signs such as:

- Just do it

- Keep the focus

- Get going

If you think a sign would help you, what would it say?

_____

_____

If a sign isn't going to do it for you, finish the statement below to find something that would help, and then go and put it into action.

I would find it easier to focus if _____

_____

This needs to be something that gets you moving when you least feel like carrying on. Whatever you choose, try it out and reconnect with what you're doing.

Another distraction from your focus is always thinking two steps ahead. We girls have to do this, actually, in order to get everything organised, but it's useful to be able either to switch it off when it's a hindrance or to have a strategy to deal with it when your multitasking gene springs into action at an inappropriate time. If you find yourself constantly coming up with things you mustn't forget to do, then make sure you keep a pen and paper by you and create a list to add to when another job pops into your mind. It means you won't forget what you've just thought of and it will help to keep you focused on what you're doing at the same time.

Another great tip for keeping you focused is to work by an open window to ensure that fresh air is flowing into the room. If you work well in silence, then keep the door shut to keep noise at bay. However, if you like working to music, then put some on in the background – but only if it's going to help. We don't want you head-banging and playing air guitar when no one's around and you're meant to be marking spelling tests!

Step 4: Prioritise

This can be another difficult area, but it is the easiest way I've found of prioritising your workload.

- Write a list of exactly what needs to be done, using bullet points, so you can see everything clearly at a glance.

- Next, decide what the deadline for each item is. Is the deadline today, tomorrow or in two days' time?

- Next, estimate how long each job will take you (in minutes).

- Start with the job with the nearest deadline and the shortest estimated completion time. Ignore every-thing else – take on that task and finish it.

- After that task, take the next job with the nearest deadline and the next shortest estimated completion time. Ignore everything else and complete that one – keep going, having regular short breaks, and your list will diminish very quickly indeed.

When you work in this way, it'll be easier to judge how long your tasks will take and you can judge when you're going to get everything finished. Quite often, the time-consuming bit is the muddle you feel in your head when you get that sense of feeling out of control and your mind goes into overdrive about how long everything will take. Before you know it, you're saying things such as, 'I'll be here for ever!' and 'I'll never finish everything.' With this plan, you'll be able realistically to identify jobs and match them to your own timetable.

Stick to this four-step rule every time you start to work. Here's a reminder:

- first, tidy up

- second, throw away

- third, keep the focus

- last, prioritise

Keep this basic sequence in your mind and you may find that you finish sooner than you thought!

The facts of life

Ever feel as if you really can't cope with what's being thrown at you? Ever feel as if you'll never take back the control? Then it's time to learn the facts of life.

No, not *those* facts! These are two very important facts that everyone should know:

- Fact No. 1: Life never throws anything at you that you're not ready to catch.
- Fact No. 2: Situations change.

Fact No. 1

Your mindset is the key to your being able to take control, not outside influences. For instance, if you're waiting for your workload to dissipate before you take back control or for your marking to decrease or your difficult class to move up a year, you will be waiting a while, because behind every batch of marking is another, and behind every exhausting class is the next one waiting to pounce. Waiting for circumstances to change before you get a life, start to smile again or sleep properly is wasted time. You have to approach things from a different angle. You have to change your mindset first. Then and only then will your workload start to ease off, your marking seem easier and your class begin to behave better.

Consider this. How differently would you run your life if you knew that life wasn't going to throw anything at you that you weren't completely capable of dealing with? What difference to your temper, your personality or your health would the knowledge of that fact make? Quite a difference, I'm sure. The thing about this fact is that you have to believe it *before* anything will change. How does it work? Well, it's all to do with your fantastic subconscious mind. You have to tell it what you want it to do. So, if you tell it, 'I'm never going to cope' or 'This is as much as I can take', that's exactly what you'll feel and exactly what will happen. You have to expand the possibility of what you currently consider to be realistic and mull those expanded possibilities over in your mind until you're absolutely comfortable with them. Then and only then will they become reality; in effect, you'll grow into them.

The only real way to feel the difference is by trying this for yourself. So, if you're up for a bit of a challenge, revamp your thoughts for at least two weeks and then look back and notice the difference. The difference may be subtle but it will definitely be there. What you have to do is to retrain your natural thought patterns (easier than you think, by the way). You have to modify all your internal language and tell yourself exactly what you want to happen. Below are some sample phrases, or you could make up your own. Whatever you do, make sure those phrases are amazing – they're your future.

- I see myself in a more capable role.
- I see myself with a social life and an organised school life.
- I see myself coping with stress easily.
- I see myself making brilliant decisions.
- I see myself organising my time beautifully.

Whichever one you choose, write it down and read it often. Learn it off by heart and repeat it every time your head whizzes off into 'the world is a horrible place' mode!

Fact No. 2

Things do change, people do see things differently with time, tempers do calm down and the human body and brain adapt to new or difficult situations brilliantly. You just have to trust that that it is what is going to happen and then you can slump in your chair and breathe out for five minutes! There's no need to hold your breath, walk around with your shoulders up by your ears or have knots in your stomach that refuse to go away. Every time you get these feelings tell yourself that things do and will change – it's just the law of averages.

No situation stays the same for very long. Even subtle or tiny changes can make substantial differences in how you feel about something, so, if you're going through a difficult period at the moment, tell yourself that things will change. It's also true that, with positive thinking and a good plan behind you, you can change them sooner than they would naturally have changed. When you tell yourself that you *can* do something, you then become clearer in your mind, less fractious and more able to make a plan of action.

Another tip to help you deal with difficult situations is to try mentally to note a time in the future by when things will have changed. For instance, if you know that by this time next week it, whatever it is, will all be over, then mentally you can benchmark a change in situation, something to aim for. If you know that you just have to get through the next half-term and that you're going to make one almighty effort to cope brilliantly and be more productive than you've ever been, it'll get you through, knowing that when it's all over you can treat yourself. It's like the carrot-and-stick thing. Give yourself a treat for getting through. It's not such a daft idea. Children work well with carrots and sticks, so at what age do they no longer work? They don't *stop* working: they *keep* working. So treat yourself for getting to the end and mark it in some way. It'll be significant to know that a difficult situation has passed and will give you a chance to turn over a fresh leaf.

Honestly, life never gives you something you're not capable of dealing with, and situations do change. You're never going to be in one particular situation for a lifetime. Live with these two facts in mind and hold your head up high – and you'll be walking on air!

Organising your paperwork to within an inch of its life!

Would you love to scale down the paperwork you possess and also feel organised enough to breeze through the rest? Here are the secrets to organising your paperwork to within an inch of its life!

OK, different people have different strengths. You know that better than anyone, and, if your major strength isn't being organised, then you'll understand just how difficult it is to pull yourself up from underneath all that clutter. You might also be aware that, if you did manage to get your systems into some kind of order, life could be much easier.

To get the very best from this tip, you'll need to have gone through the process in 'Marking among the mess!' above. The 'Marking among the mess!' tip is about clearing your space and getting rid of the rubbish, whereas this tip is more of a development on that. It's a step further and is going to help you be even more organised than you thought possible.

The old saying 'tidy desk, tidy mind' definitely has something going for it and if you knew exactly what you had among all that paperwork and knew where to lay your hands on things quickly, then you'd feel more prepared and your time spent searching for materials, papers and notes would be halved. That will leave you with a smug grin on your face in the knowledge that you've gone straight to the top of the class!

I've spoken to many teachers and teaching assistants who agree that organisation is one of their biggest problems and demotivators. Some say that it stems from never having worked in an office, so those filing systems just aren't ingrained in their psyche. Whatever your excuse, though, yes (you know what's coming), this is the time to do something about it and, the sooner you do, the sooner it'll be a delight to mark instead of a dread!

Tip No. 1

Decide which files you work best with. Visit a stationery shop and have a look at the different filing systems on offer. There are loads of different types of files and mini storage units in all sorts of different colours and patterns. You could really make your filing your own and tailor it to suit your personality.

Don't stick to boring black files: get pink, green or even yellow, and get excited about files! Make sure that, what-ever you buy, you really love them; that way you'll put papers away to your heart's content!

Tip No. 2

Get yourself two trays – an in-tray and a filing tray. In the in-tray you want to keep the pile of work you still have to action, and in the filing tray you put things that are to be filed. This way you keep your systems flowing and you should always know exactly where things are.

Tip No. 3

File often. Don't let your paperwork build up. If you've bought files that get you excited, and yes I do mean excited, you won't ever be behind again.

Tip No. 4

Name your files clearly. Use file inserts, contents pages, coloured markers, coloured dividers – they're all out there on the market to make storing your papers interesting and fun. So make use of them – and with a big fat pen. Label all your files clearly so you know what's in each one.

Tip No. 5

Last, try to keep all your files in the same place and carry around with you only what you're going to use that day. Not only does this prevent back problems, but you'll have less chance of losing important or confidential information, and it will cut down on unnecessary clutter around your home!

You work where?

If you spend more time trying to find things and collating the various bits of work scattered around your house, office and car than you do actually working, you'll be the first one to admit to panicking when asked to find anything. Use this tip to look at your workspace.

The teachers I've spoken to have all admitted to keeping their books, materials and marking in all kinds of strange places. Generally, they spread themselves out over every area of their lives, from school offices (if they have one) to the boots of their cars and even their bathrooms! If that's you, it's no wonder you're feeling frustrated, unable to cope and as if you can never get away from school! Below are some common problem areas for teachers and why they're so bad for your mood and work–life balance:

Your car

If the boot of your car is never empty of boxes and equipment for school and you can't give anyone a lift anywhere because the back seat hasn't been seen in years, then this is an area of your life that needs looking at immediately. Your car may be your primary place to keep your school work but, if you simply drive around with all of your work-load and never find the time to actually tackle it, then it's not working for you!

Not only is it not working for you, but also it'll be serving as a constant reminder of how disorganised you are, which will have a negative effect on your outlook in all kinds of areas of your life. If you think that driving your work around with you is productive or useful then, you have to ask yourself the following questions.

- Does it work?
- What effect is your littered car having on your social life and family life?
- Do your children or friends constantly complain that there's nowhere to sit?

When you take friends or family out for the day, your marking will just make you feel guilty for not working. By keeping your work in your car, you'll just end up feeling inadequate every time you drive somewhere because your unfinished work slaps you in the face – hard! It's time to find another, more suitable, place to store your papers.

Your dining room

Yes, the same goes for your dining room. Your dining room needs to be a place where your family connect each day, where you can all sit and eat together, making conversation and laugh about your stresses.

Staring at your workload over dinner is the quickest way to develop indigestion. Mealtimes are supposed to be quality time for families to catch up with each other, so, even if you need to use the dining room table as a desk during the evening, make sure you clear away all traces before you eat your meals.

Your bedroom

No, I'm not kidding, and, if you're smiling, then you'll probably have a box or two in the corner of your bedroom, too! Girls, the bedroom is a place of safety, a place to relax and be intimate with your partner, a place for morning cuddles with your children. Don't let your work creep in here ruining that precious time. If you do, you'll find it harder to sleep, harder to switch off and definitely harder to get into sexy mode with your other half!

Your lounge

Again, if your lounge is the only area for you to work, make sure you put your work away when you've finished. There's nothing worse than unfinished work in the corner of your eye screaming obscenities at you while you try to destress and catch up with your favourite soap. You'll be laden with guilt!

Your kitchen table

The kitchen table is a favourite place for working. It's probably quite central and near the kettle, too! The kitchen may, however, feel more like Piccadilly Circus than a haven for concentration. Again, if this is your only available workspace, don't let mounds of paperwork build up. Put out only what you need and then clear the table when you've finished, or, as with a bowl full of dirty washing-up, your stomach will knot up the minute you come downstairs in the morning and spot the mess.

Your bathroom

Yep, some teachers I've spoken to even have mountains of work in their bathrooms, explaining that they are most relaxed in the bath and can do background reading while relaxing. I beg to differ! Apart from the obvious danger of dropping your work into a tub full of bubbles, your bathroom is meant to be somewhere relaxing, where you let your mind drift and your shoulders drop as you lie neck deep in warm water. It's not an area to be overtaken by work and school. There has to be a cut-off point somewhere, and this is definitely it, girls!

The plan, then? Decide where you work and work only there! Seriously, when you work all over your house, car and school, you'll lose things and never feel in control of your paperwork. Choose just one place to keep your workload and keep everything in that one place, where all your things are to hand and you know exactly what you have in your possession. This needs to be somewhere that you consider to be your place of work and *not* your personal space. Not everyone has the luxury of an office and can shut the door at home time; but, wherever you work, you do need to signify *when* you're at work and when you're not, so these questions will help you identify where your best marking area is.

Where do you feel most relaxed working?

_____

_____

Where do you work most productively?

_____

_____

If you were totally organised in that place, what would it look like?

_____

_____

What actions do you need to take in order to turn your ideal working space into an organised sanctuary?

_____

_____

What rules do you need to put in place to stop your work-place overtaking your home space?

_____

_____

Wherever you decide to work, be happy there. Make sure you can concentrate and be organised. Keep out only what you're working on at the time and, most of all, protect your personal space and 'off-work' time – it's very precious!

Switching off

Do you end up laughing out loud in despair when someone suggests getting a work–life balance? It's tough to juggle it all – but not impossible.

We've already spoken about an on/off switch for your partner and family in 'And then she said …', but this tip uses boundaries as a strategy to creating a healthy work–life balance. This strategy will help you identify when you're officially off duty.

When your working life encroaches on your home life and there seems to be no clear definition, it's because there are no boundaries. I have mentioned the importance of boundaries before in other books I've written and I cannot emphasise enough the importance for teachers of observing those boundaries properly. You're used to working with them, you probably have firm boundaries in place in the classroom – but, if you're working late into the night exhausting yourself and depleting your energy, if you're marking while cooking the kids' meals and listening to your mum on the phone at the same time (yes, women multitask!), then you could probably use a few!

It's essential to have routine and structure outside the classroom and some time during the day that indicates to you and those around you that you're at home and not at work. It may be that, as soon as you walk in the door, for instance, you have to be in mum or partner mode, get the dinner organised or sort out your own children's home-work. Whoever is demanding your attention at that minute, make sure they have it. You can put boundaries in place by telling your family that at a certain time you're going to have to do some work, but, until then, your focus is on them. Your family need to know they have their mum and your partner needs to know they have you, too, and that your mind, as well as your body, is present and focused on them.

If you had boundaries at home concerning where and when you worked, what would they be? These are rules if you like, rules that your family know about and that work with your routine. There's no use in putting impossible boundaries in place. They simply won't be adhered to and will cause arguments. But a few *simple* boundaries that everyone understands will help you to take back control and start to define your role in and out of the classroom. Take a minute to answer the following questions and come up with some boundaries to try that could work with your family and your routine.

If I put a boundary in place today, what would be needed most urgently?

_____

_____

If there were a set time every night or every morning when I worked, what time would it be? (Please try when answering this question to bear in mind how your natural body clock works, as we discussed in 'You are what you sleep' above.)

_____

_____

Where do I need to work at home that least interferes with my family life?

_____

_____

How long can I concentrate before I'll need a break?

_____

_____

At what time of night will I put everything away and create some personal time?

_____

_____

What do I need to do to signify that I've finished my work for the day?

_____

_____

For that last question, I have a few tips. You could, for instance, have a shower or bath to signify that you've finished work. Some teachers feel as though they're washing the stress away. If you have a separate room to work in at home, you can shut to door to signify you've left work officially. You could even put up a closed/open sign on the door and turn it around when you leave! You could bargain with your children that, if they let you work for a few hours, you'll read them a bedtime story before they go to sleep and then that time for you could signify that you've left work, too.

Don't forget that boundaries work only if you're prepared to make them and not break them. They're not there to *stop* you from being productive: they're there to help make you *more* productive and split up your time usefully. Try them for a fortnight and see. If they've not worked, don't give up on them: just alter them and come up with different boundaries that are more likely to fit in with your schedule. And do make sure that everyone knows about your boundaries. You could even write them down somewhere so no one can forget!

How to motivate yourself to get back to work

Do you wonder how you'll gather the enthusiasm to get back to school after the holidays? Are you worried that last year's problems are just sitting there waiting for you? Then the school uniform and stationery adverts will do nothing to help – but this may.

Six weeks, even if you have spent some of that holiday time at school, is still a long time to be away from teaching. It can make getting yourself motivated again for the start of the next term quite difficult sometimes. For some, going back to school is simply a habit – it's a way of life. After all, if a teacher has been teaching for twenty years, they've pretty much been at school since they were five years old! That's a long time, and, if you love your profession and feel rested after your break, you'll be raring to go.

If not, though, how on earth do you motivate yourself? Well, that depends entirely on the reasons behind why it's hard for you to return to work. Here are the top five reasons for feeling unsettled about returning to the classroom, together with some questions for you to think about that may help. Choose the scenario that most suits your situation and think carefully before answering the questions that go with the problem. This could well be the answer.

Scenario 1: You feel disorganised at home

When you start recognising that the thought of going back to work is playing on your mind and you think that it's because you feel disorganised at home, write a list of everything that you had wanted to achieve before you went back to school.

If these things aren't planned or written down, they can easily get forgotten until you're about to walk out of the front door on your first day back and suddenly think of everything you meant to do during your time off. Writing things down will help to keep those tasks in your mind and will mean you're more likely to get them done. If the list is overwhelming, choose just three things that you couldn't live without achieving, and, if time isn't on your side, think of someone who'd be prepared to help you. You'll be surprised at just how far bribery goes!

Get your top three things achieved if nothing else, and going back to school will seem much more manageable.

Scenario 2: You're tense about a colleague you worked with last year

It's not always possible to get on with everyone, and, if a clash of personalities has left you with a tricky situation or a difficult atmosphere, walking into school could be very uncomfortable. Talk yourself through these questions and they'll give you a different emotional spin on the situation. You don't have to grin and bear it, you know: you can choose to do something about it.

If just one problem was sorted out between the two of you, what would that problem be and what kind of positive knock-on effect would that have on everything else?

_____

_____

If you've already tried to deal with the situation but your plan didn't work, write down exactly what you did.

_____

_____

Now write down the exact opposite of the above. Sometimes doing something totally out of character, doing something unexpected or reacting in a completely different way really works!

_____

_____

What is your body language like around this person?

_____

_____

If you weren't worried about this person, list three ways your body language would be different:

1. _____

2. _____

3. _____

What do you need to say to yourself to make going back to school really easy?

_____

_____

Scenario 3: You don't get on with your head and feel as if you're waiting for 'something to happen'

The agony of waiting for someone to call you into their office will take you right back in time to when you were waiting outside the head's office as a child, and most of us have been there! The best way to tackle this situation is by taking control. The best way to do that is by requesting a meeting yourself and being completely honest.

No one can slate you for asking for a meeting and starting a conversation by saying, 'I've been feeling uncomfortable ...' or 'I'd really like to know how to improve ...' Taking the bull by the horns may even go in your favour. After all, if you're the one calling the meeting, you're more likely to be prepared. Don't wait for someone else to call the shots – you can call them too!

Scenario 4: Last year, you let your workload and stress get on top of you; now you feel rested and don't want to launch straight back into those unhealthy old habits

This is very common, not only for teachers but women in all kinds of jobs after they've had a holiday. You know that, at the end of last term, you were exhausted and your family and your health may well have suffered, so now's the time to think about how you can avoid that situation again. Answering the following questions will help direct your thinking positively and will give you a couple of strategies to put in place for protection.

What specifically got you very stressed last term?

_____

_____

What could you have done to halve that stress?

_____

_____

What have you learned from last term?

_____

_____

How can you make this year extra special for you and your class?

_____

_____

Which two actions are you going to carry out this year that will make it a pleasure to go back to work?

1. _____

2. _____

Scenario 5: If you've lost the buzz that being a teacher brought and you need a change of direction

There may be any number of reasons why you feel as though you need a change of direction, but, if you think you need to rethink where your life is heading and the classroom no longer feels right, then this could be an ideal time to reconsider the structure in your life. Answer these questions to stimulate your thoughts.

If your life was totally different, what would you be doing with your time?

_____

_____

What would be your favourite hobby?

_____

_____

What would be the most exciting thing you'd be doing this week?

_____

_____

How could you start to incorporate those things into your life now?

_____

_____

If you need to rethink your finances to help make the above possible, what would you need to do?

_____

_____

If you are positive, however, that none of the above is realistic or feasible, it might help to identify the cause of your wanting to leave teaching with these questions.

What exactly is the basic problem?

_____

_____

Imagine that problem is solved and that you now enjoy being back in the classroom. Think back to the first step you took to resolve the situation.

_____

_____

With that in mind, what one thing can you do today that will help you feel more enthusiastic about going back to school?

_____

_____

Whatever's holding you back about returning to school, the strategy itself is simple. First identify the problem, then put a positive plan of action into practice. You'll feel a weight off your shoulders and going back will be much easier than you thought.

The 9 p.m. stop organiser

Is every morning a rush to get out of the door? Do you find yourself halfway to work and then realise that you've forgotten to put out the rubbish (again), didn't pick up a book you needed or have to go all the way back home for the homework?

If any of the above situations fit you, you might like to read Tina's story. Tina isn't a teacher but she is a very busy mum, pregnant, at the time of writing, with her second child and running a busy company with her husband. Tina came to see me because she felt out of control, completely disorganised, worried that she'd miss something important and as if she were drowning under her workload – the kind of feeling that many teachers face every Monday morning!

During one of her sessions, we came up with the 9 p.m. 'stop organiser'. What you have to do is stop whatever you're doing at 9 p.m. and prepare for tomorrow. Overleaf is a checklist of what you can do to make sure you're never

stumbling out of the door in the morning forgetting something important again!

- Look ahead in your diary and work out where you
  need to be and what you need to have with you for
  the next day.

- Write down what you need and then get all your
  belongings together and put them by the front door.

- Have in your mind the time you need to get up and
  the time you need to be out of the door tomorrow. If
  you need to set your alarm for a certain time, use this
  time to do that, too.

- You can also use this time to make sandwiches
  for the next day, organise what you're going to eat
  and get school bags ready, both yours and your
  children's.

It shouldn't take long – allocate just fifteen minutes to this
and then carry on with the rest of your evening. It isn't
meant to disrupt your evening, so don't spend an hour on
it. It's just a specific time that you'll be able to build into
your routine to get yourself organised. If it helps, get the
family to assist, turn the television off for fifteen minutes
and get organised. The above works very well for Monday

through Saturday, but Sunday's 9 p.m. stop organiser can be used a bit differently.

Sunday's 9 p.m. stop organiser

This is your chance to have a snapshot of the whole week ahead and schedule in any planning that you need to do to make the week run smoothly. This is the looking-from-above type of planning, where you become the manager in your own life instead of just the worker. This will mean that you're always two steps ahead of yourself and feel even more in control of your week and your workload.

Helpful tip

As well as using this time to prepare your actions, you could also use it to prepare your thoughts. This involves writing down a special word to repeat to yourself tomorrow morning if there is anything you have to deal with that feels difficult or scary. This could be anything from a meeting with a colleague or parent at school to something outside work, such as a doctor's appointment that worries you or even just the fact that tomorrow will be a really hectic day and you know you're going to get through it only if you're able to stay in control.

This word can be something that will calm you when your nerves or fears get the better of you, or something that will keep you energised and focused. You could choose from the following words or make up your own. Whichever word you choose, make sure that you write it down and say it to yourself the following day over and over again. It will help. Here are some suggestions:

bold	in control
brave	organised
calm	persistent
composed	powerful
controlled	prepared
cool	relaxed
courageous	serene
daring	smiley
determined	spirited
energetic	spontaneous
fearless	tranquil
focused	vocal

This chapter is about enabling yourself to be the one in control, organising your actions and your thoughts and going to bed feeling happy and not hysterical. Your days are busy, ladies, and your commitments exacting. You demand a lot of yourself and your capabilities and this is an excellent motivator and organiser for you to try.

Courting couples

When was the last time you and your partner acted like a couple of lovesick teenagers? Do you remember the last time you spent quality time together in each other's company? Perhaps, despite being in a relationship, you're feeling detached and isolated from your partner. If so, this tip could well induce some well-earned togetherness!

It doesn't matter if you've been together for one year or ten, if the stress of your job is encroaching on your home life, the romance in your relationship could be suffering and you may be left feeling isolated and alone. Maybe you know that you haven't been giving your partner enough attention recently, or maybe your partner's picked up this book and has flicked it open at this page and is worried that your relationship may be at risk.

I've spoken to several teachers who, in their quiet and more reflective moments, wonder whether their marriages would have lasted if only they'd done a different job. If you're concerned that you could be thinking this in a few years' time, decide to do something about it today and read on.

The importance of visualisation

I've mentioned in the earlier chapter 'Relax kids' how visualisation and relaxation exercises are wonderful at promoting wellbeing, calm and confidence in children. But I've come up with my own version for you, the teacher. This is something that your partner can read to you to help you relax. Visualisation, especially when done with your partner, promotes a sense of togetherness, security and complete relaxation. This is what you have to do.

First, try to relax as much as possible with a warm bath or a hot drink, making sure that you are both there and both feeling relaxed. Cuddle up together and make sure you are leaning against your partner. Sometimes when you drift off into a relaxed visualisation, you can feel a little disoriented, so it's reassuring to be leaning on someone for support. Perhaps your head could rest on their shoulder, their arm could be around you or you could be holding hands, whatever feels comfortable – but do make sure that you have some physical contact.

Now close your eyes and ask your partner to read the following to you, in a calm and soothing voice.

> Take a deep breath. Concentrate on your breathing and know that, with each breath, you are feeling more and more relaxed. Feel the contact with me and know that you're safe to relax, that everything is OK and I am here with you. Imagine that we are somewhere warm and secure, somewhere restful where we have a life without worries or anxiety. Imagine that we're together and happy with no constraints on time. Picture us laughing, walking hand in hand and enjoying the relaxation.
>
> You sense a deep peace and togetherness and, the more relaxed you feel, the more love you feel. Imagine that you feel beautiful and perfect and know that I love you for being beautiful and perfect and exactly the person you are now. Know that we can come back to this place of rest whenever we choose and that it's our place, completely secluded from the rest of the world. This will now be our place to relax and be together, to laugh and feel connected. We are safe, we are warm and we are together.

Let yourself drift off to sleep and ask your partner not to bring you back to being fully awake, but just let you gently slip off into sleep. It's so important to create a space for you and your partner to be together, not just in the sexual sense but in an emotional sense, so you feel connected. It's easy to let stress and tension cloud the reason you fell in love in the first place. With a bit of practice, it is also possible to conjure up that secret place in your mind when you're especially tense at work. It will help to reconnect you with your partner, even though you're not physically together, and will remind you that there are other important things in your life, not just work.

Do make sure you read this to your partner as well. This is to help both of you feel loved and wanted, and I suspect that, despite any vibes to the contrary that your partner likes to give off, they'll need a little R & R too!

The importance of touch

When you first got together, there were probably lots of touches, cuddles, kissing and hand-holding, and, over time, it does slip. It's natural to a certain extent, since it's impossible to live with that first flush of romance for ever. When the stress from your jobs creeps in and children come along, there suddenly seem to be more important things on your mind than remembering to make sure your partner feels loved and cherished! But, girls, this is important. It's vital for both of you. Even if you've been kept awake all night with crying children and have the dinner to cook, it's imperative to be tactile. Couples need to feel connected and to know that they're still on the same emotional wavelength.

It doesn't have to be anything other than having your hair stroked or having your partner drawing circles in the palm of your hand while you watch TV together. You could give your partner a head massage – or even just a hand on a shoulder when it's obvious that one of you is harassed is enough of a gesture to be soothing. These things mean a lot and it's really important that, if your other half isn't the touchy-feely, hand-holding-in-public type of person, they know that you need the reassurance of their presence.

Touching induces a deep sense of calm and trust that someone else is there and you're not alone. The action speaks volumes and your partner will definitely be earning a few brownie points for taking heed of this tip! Oh, if only they knew how many brownie points an arm around a shoulder was worth! Maybe you should put a brownie-point chart up on the wall so you literally spell it out? Head massage = 3 brownie points; foot massage = 5 brownie points; a cuddle 6 = brownie points ... You never know: points could mean prizes, as the old saying goes, and what would the prize be? I'll leave you to discuss that one, girls!

The building-block game

Do you wander round with a slightly dazed look on your face as your to-do list all blurs into one big problem? Do you panic every time you have to transfer the same jobs, week after week, on to your latest to-do list, knowing that you probably won't get the time to do them? Then rip them up and throw them away. Try the building-block game instead!

Now, we girls are famous for our to-do lists and, if you pride yourself on being the queen of all list makers, you'll know that, when it all mounts up, there is a feeling of fear that builds up as you realise that, even if you worked without sleep for a week, you'd never get through the whole list. You'll know better than anyone that not all items on your to-do list can be done instantly. Isn't it annoying when you're waiting for an answer from someone or something else to happen first before you can move on? It's just fact that a to-do list sometimes has to be done in a certain order and the anxiety of not being able to tick off those boxes as quickly as you'd like can cause excruciating frustration. If you get caught up in the confusion of what to do first, then this exercise will help. This, ladies, is not your average, run-of-the-mill to-do list, but a what-to-do-first list – there's a difference!

Consider this. How do you build up a tower of blocks? You start with the bottom block, then put the next one on top and continue until the tower is as high as you need it to be. However, it's the order of the bricks that is important for a strong structure to be built. For instance, you wouldn't start with the smallest brick at the bottom and then try to balance the very biggest and heaviest on the top, would you? No, everything would collapse! Well the same goes for your personality and temper – it all collapses if things aren't done in the right order. Try to bear that in mind when you look at the tower below.

On the next page is an example of how to use it. First of all write out your to-do list. Then start with the bottom block and ask yourself 'What needs to happen first?' or 'What do I need to do first?' Fill in the blocks one by one, working from the bottom, allocating the bricks in the order that they should be done in.

Mary-Anne used the building-block game to refine her to-do list and now she always uses this method, because

I can go to the meeting with confidence knowing what I'm walking into.

I can organise to send a letter home with the child about next week's meeting.

When I have the information I need about the parents, I can structure what I say to them next week.

Now I'm picking up Mary to take her to the meeting, I can ask her about one of the parents when she's in the car.

Now I know babysitter can pick up the children, I can pick up Mary to take her to her meeting.

Phone babysitter to ask if she's available to pick up children.

she found it worked very effectively. Mary-Anne, like many teachers, has school commitments, after-school clubs and home commitments, and she tries to help out other mums whenever she can. She had previously tried all sorts of measures to help reduce her lists and prioritise her jobs. She'd even given up using a list for a few weeks but soon she found herself writing everything down again in a bid to feel in control.

What she had never tried, though, was the building-block game, so she agreed to use it for a month to see if it was a method she could stick to, that would help her be more effective. Yes, it worked. Mary-Anne now categorises things in the order they need to happen and so even the items that were previously just being transferred from one list to the next are now actually being done. She also finds it much easier to wipe unnecessary things off her list by using this exercise.

This is a much more organised way of controlling what you have to do. Try this and you'll never look at a to-do list in quite the same way again.

Are you really listening?

Do you sometimes feel as if you're working in 'robot mode', that you have no time to think or listen to what your body or mind needs? If so, this is definitely one to read.

When I met Eileen, she walked into my office with a bright and cheery glow. She commented on the décor of my house, how well cared for and friendly my dogs were and how my directions were faultless. Eileen was funny and excited about what she'd heard both about coaching and about me. I made coffee while we chatted enthusiastically about everything from the weather to her mother.

When we moved into my office and sat down, though, with no warning, she put her head in her hands and tears rolled down her face. With the door closed and just the two of us, there were no other distractions and she knew she had to get down to the serious business of who was hiding behind her sparkling personality and radiant smile. She knew we were about to uncover the reason why she had come to be coached and why on earth this seemingly bubbly, enthusiastic and lovely lady was now crying in my office.

Eileen started to tell me about her life, which, by the way, she loves. She has a husband and family she adores, a job she loves and friends who care about her. Her house is one great merry-go-round of people coming and going, hustle and bustle. Bliss, one might think from the outside, but, unfortunately, the only way she got through it all, she explained, was to listen to everyone except herself.

Eileen felt awfully guilty even saying there was a problem with her life when she knew other women who didn't have the same kind of support. But, even so, she was sad and tired, and, when I asked what was missing, she told me she lacked the skill to listen to herself. She listened to everyone else – her class, her children, her husband, her friends – but she never stopped to hear her own voice. She walked around her life with such vigour and cheerfulness that no one realised how she'd been feeling underneath, not even her husband.

We all think we listen all of the time. It's probably perceived as one of the easiest things to do, but we're wrong. Listening is an art. Most teachers listen very well. They use silence skilfully in order to give someone space to form their answer or opinion. They always know whether or not a child is telling the truth, as they listen 'in between the lines' to what isn't being said as well as what is.

However, listening to yourself and to your body is the subject of this tip and this skill is entirely different again. It's about being more intuitive and developing a keen sense of what your needs are. If, for instance, you keep thinking, 'I need a holiday' or 'I need to cut down', then that's probably what your body is trying to tell you. However, if you sail through life ignoring your body and what it's asking for, you'll probably feel worse and worse until you end up having to take a break or stop everything you are doing. This is the reality and, much as we push ourselves to keep going, we can't just *keep* pushing. It's really important to listen to what you need and, if you follow your body's advice, it will lead you in the right direction.

Eileen used that coaching session with me as space to be listened to – but also to listen to herself. Sometimes, it's only when we vocalise our feelings, when someone is really listening to us, that we actually get the chance to hear those words, sometimes for the very first time. Eileen decided at that session that she needed to rest. If her body could talk, she told me, it would desperately want her to stop moving, walk more slowly, speak more slowly and loosen up.

This may be a strange question but it's a valuable one. Eileen confided that she'd always wanted to go to a health retreat somewhere on her own, but, of course, with a demanding job and a family, she'd never before considered the possibility of going away alone for a night. After all, she was a responsible mum, and responsible mums just don't do that – do they?

A friend of hers sprang to mind who did exactly that, though. Her friend had a holiday abroad with a girlfriend every year. Her family didn't seem to mind and her husband seemed to manage perfectly well, so why wasn't Eileen able to do the same? Why wasn't she giving herself the same attention and listening to herself in the same way as her friend? She had no answer but she did know that she needed to get away, by herself. Eileen didn't have marriage problems and she wasn't escaping just to plot when to move out. She just needed silence and to listen to her body. I'd love you to be able to allow yourself to do the same.

If you sat down in the quiet and listened to what you needed, if you listened to your intuition, what do you think your body would say? Here's your chance to find out. First of all, think where would be a good place to answer these questions. Maybe in bed when the rest of the house is asleep? Maybe on a Saturday morning while you're waiting for your child's ballet lesson to finish and you're sitting outside in the car? Think about where you need to be to concentrate for just a few minutes on these questions, then take yourself through the following one by one. Make sure you are really listening to the answers your mind first comes up with.

What do you need?

_____

_____

If your body could talk, what would it say?

_____

_____

If you had silence to think, what would you be thinking?

_____

_____

If someone listened to you, what would you say?

_____

_____

Ladies, you listen all day and probably all evening, too, so make sure that some of the time you're listening to yourself and take notice of what you're hearing. As one famous advert suggests, 'You're worth it!'

H is for health

Do you feel completely run down and exhausted for most of the time? Do you catch every bug going? Perhaps you know that you are most emotional around the time of your period and that you may have premenstrual tension. Then H is for health – and here are a couple of very helpful tips.

One of the big problems for teachers in primary schools concerns health issues. Children pick up various infections all the time and, if you're a teacher who spends all day every day with children, you're likely to catch all those lovely germs, too! It's common knowledge that a teacher in her first year is probably more at risk of catching everything going than a teacher who's spent twenty years in the class-room and built up a cast-iron resistance – but this chapter isn't just about bugs, since there are other health factors too.

It's important to keep your immune system strong, but back complaints are also commonplace, from hours spent leaning over tiny chairs giving children extra attention.

Then, of course, just because we're girls, there are all those lovely hormones running around our bodies and, if your mood swings are unpredictable and you feel especially grotty every month, PMT could be the cause. Here are a couple of tips to keep you as healthy as possible on the job.

Immune system

While it's true that everyone needs a little bit of dirt to keep their immune systems strong, it makes sense to make washing hands a frequent routine for both the children in your class and you. Many primary school classrooms have sinks, so putting an antibacterial soap cleanser next to the sink will remind everyone to wash their hands properly. As in hospitals, it's important to keep washing little hands. After all, runny noses get wiped, children hug each other all the time and often go to the toilet without remembering to wash their hands. As teacher, you probably already remind children a million times a day to wash their hands, but yours are important, too, since toys, books and surfaces all hide bacteria that can cause illness, so be scrupulously clean and it should help.

Of course, you can't mention immune systems without linking it to what we eat. The nutritionist and author of *Wonderfoods* (2006, Quadrille Publishing), Natalie Savona, explains, 'You have to remember it's not just being exposed to the bugs that is the issue but it's also about keeping your body in as good a state as you can, so that when the bugs land they've got a minimal chance of surviving and making you ill.' According to Natalie, there are two main things to consider. 'Firstly, things that undermine your immunity: if you drink too much alcohol, if you're a smoker, if you're stressed or if you're not sleeping well, you are more susceptible to infection. Secondly, things that boost your defences: resting well and eating well. Obvious as it may seem, it's important to have a varied diet which includes five lots of fruit and vegetables a day, as they really are particularly good sources of vitamins and minerals.'

If you think your immune system could still do with a boost, though, Natalie recommends vitamin C, along with a multivitamin that contains zinc, all of which are available from your local health-food shop. 'A good anti-oxidant blend,' Natalie continues, 'is also important for the health of your immune system and it gives your liver a boost too.'

Back problems

It's no wonder you get home at the end of the day with backache that makes you irritable, tense and uncomfortable, if you've spent all day leaning over small chairs and carrying around loads of books on your hips as if they were small children. If that's you, you'll find these top tips from state-registered physiotherapist Kirsten Nutman a massive help.

1. Avoid twisting your back at all times.

2. Carry things as close to the front of the body as possible using both your arms.

3. One heavy bag should be split into two smaller bags so that you carry one on each arm to distribute the weight evenly.

4. When standing up to teach, make sure you use your abdominal muscles to hold your body up. That means tightening tummy and bottom muscles. This keeps the arch in the small of the back to a minimum. If when you stand, your back is arched excessively, you'll be putting a great deal of strain on it.

5. Don't remain in any one position for a long period of time. Change your standing or sitting position regularly, especially if you already suffer from back pain.

6. When bending down to little chairs, squat by bending from the knees to keep the natural curve in the spine. Alternatively, kneel if you are able and keep the back straight when you do so.

Of course, you could try looking at the subject of lifting and carrying in a whole new light. John Carpmael, an Alexander technique practitioner, describes how the Alexander technique might help by observing what is really going on. He says,

> All of us spend the majority of our lives running on autopilot. We don't really know what we are doing – we just let our habits take us through the daily routines. So, when we are about to lift a bag, the first thing we need to do is to wake up to the fact that we are being run by our habit. The next thing is to allow ourselves the luxury of noticing what exactly that habit is – so we can begin to act almost as witnesses to the simple details of our lives.
>
> We notice what we do; we notice how we feel while we do it; we notice what we are thinking while we are doing it; we notice what happens to our vision, our hearing, our sense

of touch and so on, while we do what we do. That noticing doesn't have to be judgemental ('Oh, I'm doing it all wrong') – it can be interested ('Wow, I never noticed that before!'). Sometimes it is easier to do this in terms of other people. Have a look at how other people go about picking up a bag. You will be amazed at how many different ways there are to carry out this simple activity. So now we are awake and noticing with interest.

The next thing is to invite something new and unexpected into this routine activity which has become so hackneyed and tired. We don't know what the new thing will be – that's the point: it's supposed to be something new! So you say to yourself, 'I want something new, different and unexpected – something that is more appropriate for me.'

At this point we can start to look for a new and more rational approach to picking up a bag. What we currently do is pure habit – it is what I learned to do at some time in the past. What would an anatomist or a physiologist suggest? How about an engineer? Would it make sense to bend my knees when lifting, and, if so, why? Would it be better for me to carry the weight on my left or my right side, or maybe spread the weight? How about making more than one trip carrying lighter loads?

If we were looking at something other than lifting a bag, we would ask different questions but the process would be similar. Once we have come up with a possible new strategy, then we can try it out. Maybe it will work; maybe it won't. Either way, we win because now we know something more about ourselves, and we have refreshed our habit with an input of something new and spontaneous. But it is important to be aware that habit is very strong and that it will always tend to reassert itself, which means that we need to continue to go through this whole process, time after time after time.

What John has described is a very boiled-down version of the Alexander technique. It sounds simple but habit is very strong and will reassert itself no matter what good resolutions we may have, which is why it may be helpful to take lessons from a qualified teacher. The Society of Teachers of the Alexander Technique can locate a teacher near you.

PMT

It's very easy to blame the slightest temper tantrum (and, yes, we adults get them as well as the kids) on the time of the month, but, if you think your PMT is worse than usual, there are several things you can do. Visit the doctor if that's your preferred course of action or arrange an appointment with a recommended complementary health practitioner, such as a homoeopath, who can help enormously, a reflexologist or a kinesiologist for a treatment. Gone are the days when PMT has to be suffered in silence. Natalie Savona says that smoking, drinking alcohol and a poor diet all contribute to making PMT worse, but a supplement of vitamin B complex and GLA (gamma-linolenic acid) from your local health-food shop can be a great help, alongside a good diet. These supplements generally need to be taken regularly for a couple of months before you notice an effect, but do try them and see. You could be feeling like a different woman before you know it!

Pat is a prime example of how the symptoms of PMT can be helped with a supplement. Every month her husband knew that she was about to start her period before she did! She'd turn from a patient, kind and polite person into an angry, impatient and tearful wreck! She scared herself one day when a young child made her jump, quite by accident, and she shouted until she made the child cry! So appalled was she by her own behaviour that she marched into a health-food shop later that day and explained her symptoms to the assistant, who gave her capsules of evening primrose oil and said with a smile, 'Take these for at least two months and you'll feel like a new woman!'

She did. Religiously. Every evening, she took her tablet – and the assistant was right: it did take two months. Now she has to look at the calendar to check her dates, since she's even-tempered and has none of the old backaches or stomach pains, and both she and her husband are relieved!

This is all good advice, ladies, so try it for yourselves!

Sprinkling optimism

Feeling drained by someone else's negativity? Do you feel as if you're wading through treacle to get people to look on the upside? Then this could help you to ward off those negative nasties.

Here's the scenario. You're generally a positive person and, in a crisis, you're always a glass-half-full type without a bad word to say about anyone. You're always encouraging people to think the best of themselves and you're the first one to stick up for the downtrodden one in an argument. You live by the innocent-until-proven-guilty theory and, even if they're guilty of *something*, you're still able to point out their good points!

So, why is it that you end up suffering from other people's negativity to the point where it's become a daily struggle to be the normal happy-go-lucky you that everyone loves? If you work with negative people, if you're hearing negative comments, if you're a bystander listening to bitchy conversations about other staff or, worse, the children, then this won't sit at all well with you. Before you know it, the thought of another day at school will fill you with horror.

Negativity is catching, and, if you're not protecting yourself, it's as easy to pick up as the common cold! Although there are certainly some people in this world who are naturally positive, even they will be tested to the limit if faced with a barrage of complaints and insults over their morning coffee.

Negative people do exist – in their droves! If you're anything like Helen, you could be feeling the pressure of that negativity as forcefully as if it were being deliberately thrown directly at you. Helen had been feeling ill, which wasn't usual for her. She'd been feeling sick, had lost her appetite and felt emotionally drained. This had gone on for months until her children and husband sat her down and told her they were worried. They went with her to the doctor, who could find nothing wrong. Blood tests were done and everything seemed fine. Physically she was in good health according to the nurse, so what had been going on in recent months? School was fine with no more pressure than usual, her home life was good, busy and hectic but enjoyable, her children were doing well in their education and her relationship with her husband hadn't suffered any major problems. So what on earth was causing Helen to feel so under the weather?

She worried for days about what was going on. Then, one day at school, it hit her. A major argument suddenly erupted between two colleagues in the middle of the staffroom. Very publicly, one teacher swore, threw papers and shouted, and everyone stopped what they were doing and stared at the perpetrator. Helen then realised that the woman concerned was causing her to feel so agitated that she had begun to feel ill. She also realised that this woman was always edgy, negative and moody. Following the outburst, Helen spoke to other staff about the negativity she'd been sensing and they had noticed it, too, although not to the same degree. At last Helen had found her cause. She knew that, if she was going to feel better, she had to cope more effectively with her colleague's negativity.

During a coaching session, we talked through various ways of dealing with negativity in general, not just that emanating from her colleague. Helen realised that her optimism was precious and needed protecting, so, as a solution, she came up with a magical idea for counter-acting other people's negativity. She decided that, before she left the sanctuary of her house in the morning, she would sprinkle positive dust over herself and her family, protecting them from negativity during the day.

Positive dust isn't going to change her colleague's atti- tude, so how does it help? It's the shift in *Helen's* attitude that would help and sprinkling optimism every morning made her more aware of keeping herself positive throughout the day. It gave her and her family an imaginary protection from other people's potentially harmful negative vibes. Now this won't do the trick for everyone; and, if you're not the magical, fairy-tale type of girl, then this isn't going to work. But what would? What would you need to do to protect your optimism and remind yourself that other people's moods don't have to affect yours? Write down three different ways of deflecting negativity that could work for you, then take one each week and try it out. Long-term, adopt whichever seems to work the best.

1. _____

2. _____

3. _____

Since Helen explained to her family the concept of sprink- ling optimism, her children have used it in all kinds of ways. Her son used it when he took an exam and her daughter used it for her driving test. Her husband even used it during a meeting at work and they all agreed that they felt they did better than they would have done had they allowed the nerves and negativity to kick in.

Flimsy as sprinkling magical positive dust sounds, it's a frame of mind, and it's about using that powerful subconscious of yours to bring you the results you need. All I can say is that negativity can be a debilitating energy to have to work or live with and there can't be any harm in trying a sprinkle of optimism!

Breathing fresh air

When was the last time you exercised? Are you a gym fiend or do you do anything to avoid what might get you out of breath? Exercise is far more than keeping cellulite at bay!

Now, if you're a PE teacher, you probably won't need to use this tip. However, there are an awful lot of teachers who get stuck in the trap of being too busy to exercise and, although I'm not a teacher, it's a trap I found myself in very recently. I used to be a dancer (many years ago!) and, since those heady days of flinging my legs in the air on stage every night, I've got stuck into work, running my company, writing books, getting married and enjoying far too many evenings in with a bottle of wine. The result? Not only did I discover that I had more wobbly bits than before, but I also realised I was becoming a bit stressed! Backaches, feeling irritable and getting out of breath as I climbed the stairs – they were all indications to me that perhaps this fitness lark would do me more good than just toning up the wobbly bits! So I decided to do something about it.

I went out and bought a very gorgeous new pair of trainers, got in the car and measured out a three-mile round trip where I live and promised myself faithfully that I'd go walking – speedy walking, that is, not just meandering but proper stomping! I've taken this on as a bit of a habit now and can regularly be seen storming around the block as if I were about to blow a fuse. Of course, I'm not about to blow a fuse but that's how I walk, to make a point of keeping up a pace that'll get me out of breath.

I also took some advice from Michelle Farnworth, an expert personal trainer, to help me make the most of my sessions, and I think her advice is well worth writing about. 'Walking is the ultimate destressor. It allows the mind to wander, the body to move and the soul to quieten,' says Michelle. It's not just something that gets you from A to B: it's a way of clearing the head, calming tempers, letting out frustration and, of course, if the odd particle of cellulite decides to pack its bags from the thighs, trust me, no girl's going to stop it!

Opposite are Michelle's top tips for walking to maximise the benefit to those thighs!

Ten top tips

1. **Frequency**: A routine of walking will allow you to achieve the most health benefits. However long you walk for, try to make it a habit, whether it's twice a week or every day.

2. **Intensity**: How fast you walk can make such a difference. If you just need some fresh air, then by all means meander at your own pace; but, if you want to burn the fat, try to walk at a brisk pace. Test yourself by talking: if you can talk without getting breathless, then you're going at the right speed.

3. **Time**: You don't have to walk a long way; a ten-minute walk three times a day has proved to be just as beneficial as one long walk of thirty minutes.

4. **Type**: Do you live in a flat area? Do you ever walk up hills and struggle to catch your breath once you've reached the top? Try to alternate your route, as this will challenge the body and stop the mind becoming bored. Or, instead of walking briskly all the time, integrate interval training into your walk. Challenge yourself to walk fast between two lampposts, and then easy between the next two, and so on. Changing the speed of your strides will surprise the body and in turn

you will improve both your fat-burning ability and your cardiovascular fitness.

5. **Form**: Instead of taking long strides, shorten your gait so that your body floats over your feet. This will better align your spine and hips, and stop your joints from experiencing stress. Do you normally look at the floor when you walk? Lift your head and notice the world around you!

6. **Where**: During the summer evenings escape from your usual surroundings and drive out into the country-side, to the coast or to the mountains. Really look at your surroundings. Appreciate the world around you, both man-made and natural. Be adventurous with your walking route: go somewhere you'd never normally go.

7. **Security**: You've probably heard this a million times before, but how many of us actually follow the practice of telling someone where we are going and when we expect to be back? Do it! It saves lives. Period.

8. **Footwear**: Ideally, proper walking shoes would be your first purchase but if you aren't able to buy them – for whatever reason – then, as long as your shoes are in good condition and give you good support, you

should be fine in them. An inexpensive pair of trainers from your local sports shop will be fine for pavement and trail walking. However, if you're aiming to walk off road, in mountainous areas or on the sand, you may want to treat yourself to a proper pair of walking shoes or boots.

9. **What to wear**: The main thing we women have to worry about is the effect of gravity on our chests! If you're the kind of gal who really doesn't need to worry about wearing a bra, then you can skip this point; but, if you're anything over a B cup, then you should really consider wearing a sports bra. Walking may not provide an awful lot of movement, but wouldn't you rather your chest stayed in one place than risk having it slide down your front? There are some excellent designs out there, so try many different varieties and find something that suits you.

10. **And, most importantly, have fun!**: Involve friends, family and work colleagues in walking activities. Set up a treasure hunt, go for a picnic, collect seashells, spot birds, follow animal tracks, outpace other mothers walking their children to school! The list is endless. Use the environment around you and be adventurous. Most of all, have fun – and walk with a smile.

I'm not the only one, though, to have donned my trainers and dug out my tracky bottoms. Lesley took heed and did exactly the same. She teachers Year 3 and, as is the case with most teachers, her workload seems to increase every term. She was finding that her temper as well as her body could do with a bit of control, so she took up walking every morning before school. She started by walking just a mile and then increased it in the summer when the bright mornings appeared. Six months on, if Lesley doesn't get her early morning walk, she's irritable, lethargic and even a bit resentful! She says, 'I found that building walking into my routine was easier than I thought: I just needed to get my head around what time I woke up. And I also bought a cap so I didn't need to fiddle with my hair! I don't care what I look like. I sort myself out when I get home. I'm probably a much nicer teacher to the children and I feel more together in general.'

Dawn is a teacher too and finds walking to be her instinctive response at times of stress or anxiety. It is an escape mechanism that uniquely combines the physical, sensual and emotional. It distracts the eye and the ear, heightens awareness of weather and climate and diverts the mind from its preoccupations. She also told me that she finds it especially restorative in a natural environment, when the senses become awakened by contact with the elements. Even on a wet and windy day, if you're suitably clad, walking provides an invigorating and refreshing experience that drives small irritations and preoccupations away and puts things firmly in perspective. As a parent of small sons, she found that a welly-booted walk was the best antidote to sibling squabbles, whatever the weather. She can't recommend it more highly to frazzled parents.

What more encouragement do you need, ladies? Find out what you could get from incorporating walking into your life. You might be surprised at just how different you could feel.

A little tender loving care required

Are you feeling isolated as a teacher? Do you have problems that you'd love to share with someone but don't know whom to turn to? If the only chance you get to talk to other teachers is as the kettle boils in the staffroom before you swig another coffee and run to your next class, then you could do with a little TLC.

We girls are very good at TLC, and, if you're feeling snowed under with work, lost in the stress of everything your job involves and distant from your colleagues, then you may take inspiration from Linda Westall and Angela Ward.

They're not teachers, but they are busy working women who decided to set up their own support group exclusively for women, called Women on Top (we met them in the chapter 'Self-preservation' earlier). What has this got to do with teachers? Well, far from being the same as any other support group, they recognise that women build friendships and support each other in a completely different way from men. Linda and Angela found that the usual, formal and mainly male-dominated area of business-card-swapping lunches was just not giving them the kind of support they needed, so they formed their own company, Women on Top. Within their Women on Top lunches, they run TLC sessions – and this is where you come in.

'The idea is this,' says Linda. 'Someone takes on the role of facilitator and everyone spends a few minutes thinking about the good things and/or bad things that have happened to them over the past couple of weeks. Anything they need, like a service or help with a problem that they just can't seem to find a solution for, they write down on a postcard. You have to be brave here, but the first step is actually writing it down! The cards are collected by the facilitator and read out, one by one, to the group. Then the "magic" starts to happen! Wow! There *is* someone who's had just as bad a week as you, someone who needs a product and *you* happen to know where to get it! All of a sudden, everyone is interacting, helping each other, giving and taking. Everyone feels great and at the end of the session everyone is buzzing. People who never realised they had a common problem or need start talking to each other. Depending on how many people are involved, the maximum time would be fifteen minutes.'

This is a unique way of sharing information, building friendships and giving each other a support system that plain old staffroom meetings just can't compete with. I've spoken to teachers who feel that they don't always have the support and backup they need at work and at home, so they carry their stress on their own, sometimes ending up feeling miserable as a result. Some teachers speak of staff bullying, uncomfortable atmospheres and even the perceived favouritism of certain teachers. This seems to be the atmosphere in some staffrooms and it's not conducive to relaxed or productive teaching. Now, it's important to point out that not all staffrooms feel like this, but there are certainly enough to acknowledge that there is a distinct lack of support in some of them. What is your staffroom like? Do you feel that it's a place you can comfortably go to relax, think more clearly or speak openly to colleagues? Is it a place where your colleagues are likely to notice if you're looking frazzled or tearful? If the answer is no, introducing TLC into the staffroom could bring a whole new ambience.

Bringing TLC sessions into the staffroom – even if it was for just fifteen minutes, as Linda suggests, at the beginning or end of the day or by working it around the school timetable – would mean that you're getting a network of support within your school.

'This concept would work so well in primary schools,' agrees Linda, 'because teachers, when they do grab a coffee for five minutes in the staffroom, often only talk briefly about the next lesson or how none of the children did their homework. How great would it be to sit down and spend some TLC time! This could be done on a regular basis, maybe even including other local primary schools, because you can bet your bottom dollar that other female teachers have the same issues. The most important thing about TLC is that you really get to know each other and you share your worries, concerns and your success.'

TLC sessions mean that women develop a deeper understanding of their colleagues and a sense of friend-ship and belonging. After all, you teach mainly on your own, in your own classroom, so, if you're feeling cut off or secluded at all, you could well find this a lifeline and a substantial support in your everyday school life. Why not follow Linda and Angela's lead? Be proactive and an 'A' star teacher, do your TLC homework on a regular basis.

Personal planning action

It's meant to help, it's meant to reduce your stress; but, if you're getting panicked by the fear of not using your PPA time properly, let this be your guide!

Planning, preparation and *assessment* (PPA) time – Phase 3 of the government's Workforce Remodelling initiative to help teachers deal with their workload. Its aim? To help you reduce your stress levels and create a work–life balance that's really effective. You're probably working with it in your school right now. Phase 1 of the Workforce Re-modelling scheme was to make sure that all administration tasks – photocopying, for instance – are passed from teachers to support staff. Phase 2, which is probably more suited to secondary schools than primary, is to make sure that teachers are not put in the position whereby they are covering for sick colleagues. But this tip is specifically about Phase 3.

As you'll be fully aware by now, Phase 3 means that every teacher is entitled to 10 per cent of their working week to plan and prepare. It's time that must be taken in chunks of no less than half an hour at a time. Now, every school will be different and it'll be up to you and your head to timetable in when this is best taken for you and your schedule, but, once it is, you need to be fully prepared, and this tip could mean the difference between making that time useful and making it a complete waste!

This time is not to be used on anything other than school matters, so, if it's tempting to skip off to a doctor's or dental appointment, resist the urge and work with your head to make sure you can attend at another time. This is the one time each week when you're allowed to focus directly on your workload without the interruption of children or teaching. So here is the 'when, where, what' rule that you can apply to PPA time to make sure it's used to its maximum benefit.

When

It's important to establish a routine around your PPA time, so, ideally, it should be the same time each week and in the same place to make sure that it works really well for you.

Where

We've spoken about the benefits of knowing where you work and in what environment you work best, but, particularly for this part of your day, it's really important to be sure that *where* you choose to spend that time makes the time profitable. It's no good planning to spend it in the staffroom if it's uncomfortable, there's nowhere to sit and you waste ten minutes making a drink. It's also important not to spend that time in, say, the library, if the door keeps banging because teachers or children are wandering in and out and you are repeatedly disturbed. As for finding solace near the school office, if a ringing phone winds you up, you won't be getting any work done there, girls!

If your PPA time is split up and you have several half-hour chunks, you need to be completely focused during that time and be able to sit and work somewhere that suits you. Half an hour flies by if you're not prepared for it. If you have longer periods available or your PPA time is at the beginning or end of the school day, you might like to consider whether that time might be more profitably spent at home. If you think it would, discuss it with your head. Consider the following questions and write down your answer if it's useful.

Where would be a good place for you to work?

_____

Would your PPA time be best taken at home?

_____

Do you get easily distracted by passers-by?

_____

Do you need complete silence to concentrate?

_____

It's important, also, to find somewhere that is close to where you will be needed *after* your PPA time. It's no good spending half of your designated time walking from one end of the school to another, since you'll simply lose both time and focus. If you work better with a cup of coffee on the desk, then make sure that you've made your coffee. These questions will all need your consideration if you're going to make that 10 per cent count.

If you can't find a suitable place to sit and work, it's important to let someone know. This time is meant to be valuable and profitable, so, if it doesn't work for you, don't just grumble: find out who is the best person to feed back to and let them know.

The main message here is to identify where you will work best and then protect your precious time by being ready to sit and focus.

What

We've also looked at planning your time differently in previous chapters, but it may be helpful when you plan your weekly lessons to have a little box marked 'PPA'. You could be using your PPA time differently each week, depending on your commitments and workload, so think about the following week and consider these questions to help you identify what you'll be using that precious time for.

What will you have to prepare for?

_____

What will you have to mark?

_____

What will you need with you?

_____

That's the 'when, where, what' rule taken care of, but there are two other strategies that could be very helpful in over-coming a common problem associated with PPA time. I've spoken to several teachers who are working with PPA at the moment and one of their bugbears is that other staff see them working and interrupt them! It can be very difficult to get across to someone who needs information or a chat that this is your PPA time and you desperately need to be left alone to work. You won't want to be rude and, unless you have an excuse, it can be really hard to get your point across without upsetting or offending a colleague.

There are two different ways of dealing with this. The first is to have your line ready so that, if someone comes up to talk something through with you, you can say some-thing like, 'I'd love to talk but this is my PPA time and I really need to concentrate at the moment. Can we meet later?' This can be very effective, but, if that's not you and you can't see yourself getting past the 'I'd love to' bit, then you'll love my second technique. Get some PPA IN PROGRESS tent cards made and have them readily avail-able in the staffroom. As with the RESERVED card in a restaurant, most people will avoid sitting at that table, so, when you have your PPA time, put your PPA IN PROGRESS tent card on your work station with you. It would be an extremely insensitive colleague who would interrupt you other than in an emergency. This is about respecting each other's space, and, if you think a PPA IN PROGRESS tent card would work in your school, be the one to suggest it – and you may find that your colleagues breathe a sigh of relief as well as you!

In short, you need to prepare for your PPA time really well and in advance! Identify clearly how you intend to use it and estimate how long your tasks will take to achieve. This is breathing space, ladies, so prepare 'when, where, what' and feel your stress levels dissolve!

About Lynette Allen

For more information on private coaching sessions with Lynette Allen, or speaking engagements, or to discuss a *Behind with the Marking and Plagued by Nits* workshop at your school, you can email her at:

lynette@lynetteallen.co.uk or visit www.lynetteallen.co.uk.

Perhaps you'd like to subscribe to 'Lynette's Tips'. These are short life-coaching tips for women that are emailed directly to you every fortnight with Lynette's compliments. To subscribe, simply send a blank email with the word 'SUBSCRIBE' in the subject box to lynette@lynetteallen.co.uk.

Great websites for support/resources

Relax Kids
www.relaxkids.com
For relaxing CDs to chill out children and teachers

Michelle Farnworth, personal trainer
www.michellefarnworth.com

Women on Top
www.women-on-top.com
For more information on the support group, Women on Top, and the TLC exercises

Natalie Savona, nutritionist
www.nataliesavona.com
For nutritional advice

Behaviour UK
www.behaviouruk.com
A behaviour website for children

Teacher Support Network
www.teachersupport.info
An online network for teachers

Teaching Expertise
www.teachingexpertise.com
Online help for teachers

Voice Care Network UK (VCN)
www.voicecare.org.uk
For more information about using your voice in the classroom

Dr Edward Bach Centre
www.bachcentre.com
For more information on Bach flower remedies

The Society of Teachers of the Alexander Technique
www.stat.org.uk

Lynette Allen
www.lynetteallen.co.uk
For more information on Lynette Allen, personal coaching for teachers or 'Behind with the Marking and Plagued by Nits' workshops

Behind with the Laundry and Living off Chocolate

Life changing strategies for busy women

Lynette Allen

£9.99, 208pp, paperback with CD, isbn: 1904424392

Behind with the Laundry and Living off Chocolate is for busy women of all ages and from all walks of life. Life coach Lynette Allen reveals her inspirational, intuitive and realistic tips for creating a balanced, fun, stress-free and fulfilling life. Through her own experience of getting the life she dreamed of, she offers a fresh perspective on all aspects of living. From life's crossroads, to coping with or addressing challenges, women can easily incorporate her workable tips into their day-to-day lives to create dramatic change with just a little re-programming.

"... Lynette has got us life jugglers totally sussed!"

Denyse Douglas, Columnist, Black Beauty and Hair Magazine

"Get your life moving on once and for all and see your life change overnight (promise!)."

Top Sante magazine

"... effective strategies ... Whether you're trying to lose weight, make more time for yourself or slash your stress levels"

Slimming Magazine

"Every busy woman (no, make that any woman) should follow Lynette's advice—it works!"

Charlotte Smith, Editor, Natural Health & Wellbeing magazine

Crown House Publishing Limited
www.crownhouse.co.uk

Behind with the Mortgage and Living off Plastic

Charge up your life, not your credit card

Lynette Allen

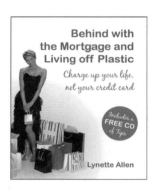

£9.99, 256pp, paperback with CD, isbn: 1904424953

For women, the underlying causes of financial problems are very often nothing to do with money and everything to do with being in charge of their lives and emotions.

When a girl feels down or troubled, a bit of retail therapy can provide a temporary salve and give them a quick lift. Then, like a sugar surge, it's back to reality as the bills pile up. Using Lynette Allen's short tips, which can be selected at random, women of any age can discover alternative and more constructive ways of getting that high and holding on to it, permanently.

Although *Behind with the Mortgage and Living off Plastic* does include strategies to help sort out a woman's finances, it is not so much a book about controlling funds as building up an inner bank of emotional resources to remove her need to spend, spend, spend.

"... follow Lynette's advice – it works!"   **Natural Health & Wellbeing magazine**

"Lynette helped me rethink my outlook on life."   **Zest magazine**

"... a fab present for a busy girlfriend who, at times, finds herself pushed to the edges of her own life."   **Spirit & Destiny magazine**

"... inspiring and heart-warming stuff."   **Health & Fitness magazine**

Crown House Publishing Limited
www.crownhouse.co.uk